ROUTLEDGE LIBRARY EDITIONS: EARLY YEARS

Volume 12

BABIES GROWING UP

BABIES GROWING UP

Their Progress From Before Birth Right Through the Nursery Years

NURSE McKAY

Routledge
Taylor & Francis Group

LONDON AND NEW YORK

First published in 1956 by Routledge & Kegan Paul Ltd

This edition first published in 2023
by Routledge
4 Park Square, Milton Park, Abingdon, Oxon OX14 4RN

and by Routledge
605 Third Avenue, New York, NY 10158

Routledge is an imprint of the Taylor & Francis Group, an informa business

British Library Cataloguing in Publication Data
A catalogue record for this book is available from the British Library

ISBN: 978-1-032-34369-3 (Set)
ISBN: 978-1-032-35846-8 (Volume 12) (hbk)
ISBN: 978-1-032-35856-7 (Volume 12) (pbk)
ISBN: 978-1-003-32899-5 (Volume 12) (ebk)

DOI: 10.4324/9781003328995

Publisher's Note
The publisher has gone to great lengths to ensure the quality of this reprint but points out that some imperfections in the original copies may be apparent.

Disclaimer
The publisher has made every effort to trace copyright holders and would welcome correspondence from those they have been unable to trace.

BABIES GROWING UP

THEIR PROGRESS FROM BEFORE BIRTH RIGHT THROUGH THE NURSERY YEARS

by

NURSE McKAY

Director of the Mothercraft Bureau
of the *Woman's Pictorial* and
Mother and Home

1956
LONDON
ROUTLEDGE & KEGAN PAUL LTD

First published in 1956
by Routledge & Kegan Paul Ltd
Broadway House
68–74 Carter Lane, London EC4
Printed in Great Britain
by Butler & Tanner Ltd
Frome and London

CONTENTS

Contents

PREFACE

To COMPRESS INTO brief yet readable form the essentials of success-
ful parentcraft is the aim of this little book. Always bearing in
mind the fourfold development of each new life—physical, mental,
emotional, spiritual.

Simply, and as completely as possible, it seeks to sum up the
essence of the mothercraft advice given over the years through the
pages of *Woman's Pictorial* and *Mother and Home*, to whose Editors
I am greatly indebted for permission to include material which has
already appeared in their journals.

I would also like to pay a warm tribute to Miss M. Liddiard,
for so many years the Nursing Director of the Mothercraft Training
Society, to whose work and teaching, I, in common with thousands
of other mothers and nurses, owe so much.

Also to Sir Frederick Truby King, C.M.G., whose selfless,
inspiring and largely pioneering work, both in New Zealand and
in this Country did so much to establish modern Mothercraft on
a sound and yet idealistic basis.

No book can hope to cover every aspect of the wide and ever-
growing problems of modern parentcraft, but suggestions for
further reading, and addresses of Societies where help is available
have been included to increase the value of the advice offered.

July 1955.   LONDON

I
GROWTH OF BABY—BEFORE BIRTH

ALL GROWTH IS interesting, but for sheer fascination nothing can equal the story of the development of an almost invisible speck into a living being of flesh and blood, with power to breathe and to take nourishment—complete down to the last eyelash and finger-nail.

Life begins when a tiny spermatozoon—so minute that it has been estimated that if the heads of two million of them were put into a husk of rice there would be room to spare—meets the larger but still quite microscopic ovum. A thimble, it is said, would hold three million ova.

At the moment of fusion the minute egg carries within its tiny compass every possible potentiality, physical and mental, of the future man or woman, and immediately a division of the cells commences which will continue with feverish activity until a perfect baby has been formed.

The rapidity of the early growth is encouraging because many mothers are under the impression that they may mar their child in one way or another by strong emotions, anxieties or accidents. Nature, however, leaves little to chance and the mother is not aware of her condition until the embryo, already several weeks old, is showing very clearly the shape of the child-to-be.

By the end of the *second lunar month*, the embryo has so unmistakable a human face, also arms and legs, with fingers, toes, elbows and knees, that he receives the label of foetus. But even a month before this, in his embryo stage, a tube which will develop into the heart is pulsating and propelling blood through microscopic arteries. He's now about one inch from head to buttocks. In this month, buds for all the milk teeth are laid down, sockets for them developing in the jaw line.

During the *third lunar month*, could we examine baby, we should be able to determine his sex. This is an important point, for sometimes emotional force is wasted in trying to 'will' a son or daughter into being. Such desires, though they can have no physical effect on the child, yet may set up psychological reactions when the longed-for-son is found to be a daughter, or vice versa.

The sex of the child is conveyed by the father's sperm though the mother is often the one blamed when a longed-for heir is delayed.

By the end of the *fourth month*, the foetus, who weighs 4 oz., would be nearly 7 in. long if its legs were extended. The skin is pink because of the presence of blood, and a fine, downy hair is growing on it.

Now the bony framework of the body is very slowly beginning to harden, starting with the spinal column and spreading throughout the greater part of the system, though some bones do not completely ossify until after birth.

By the *fifth month* the nails begin to grow. Tonsils and adenoids develop, and enamel is deposited on the milk teeth. The length is now 10 in., and the weight about 8 oz.

By the end of the *sixth month*, we have a complete baby in miniature, except for a lack of fat under the skin. The nostrils open, the liver begins to secrete bile, and the body becomes covered with a protective covering known as vernix caseosa. Length is about 12 in., and weight one and a half pounds.

By the end of the *seventh month* baby can open his eyes, and were he to be born now, he would have a one in ten chance of survival. He now starts laying in important stores of iron, building up his fat tissues, and generally improving his appearance. He gains about half a pound a week at this stage, and as he needs good building material, the mother should watch her diet and health with special care.

By the time of birth baby will be about 20 to 21 in. in length, weighing 7 to 7½ lb. The finger-nails will be firm and protrude beyond the finger-tips. Lungs, vocal chords and digestive system will all be ready to function, and once more a miracle will have taken place for those with eyes to see and imagination to wonder.

FOR FURTHER READING

Sons and Daughters, by Roger Pilkington. Allen & Unwin, 18s.
Expectant Motherhood, by Nicholas Eastman. H. K. Lewis, Ltd., 8s. 6d.

II

SIGNS OF PREGNANCY

REACTIONS TO THE profoundly moving experience of motherhood are bound to vary just because there are so many kinds of women, with so many differing degrees of health and of personality. Thus the signposts which Nature erects on the road to motherhood may not always be easy to read.

With some mothers-to-be the start of a long-desired pregnancy ushers in a sense of enhanced vitality, gaiety and happiness. Others, who have various conflicts to solve, consciously or unconsciously, before they can fully accept the situation, pass through a period of low spirits, depression, pessimism. Some note that their appetite increases, perhaps with a clamorous desire for tasty, sharp or savoury flavours. Others find that nausea so dogs their footsteps that they cannot bear to think about meals at all. From these and other diverse experiences one fact emerges—there is some deviation from the usual, in one direction or another.

Missed Period

The sign of conception having occured most usually recognized is the missing of an expected period. It is, however, possible for other causes to be operative so this cannot be conclusive. Again, in some cases the period continues for two or three months, though lessened in amount. Such losses are probably a sign of irritability of the womb amounting to a threatened miscarriage; be that as it may, it tends to confuse the issue.

(In some circumstances, pregnancy can occur without a prior menstruation, e.g. when the mother is breast-feeding, or in the case of a child marriage.)

Breast Changes

The second important sign is connected with changes in the breasts. These are so closely linked to the reproductive system and have so

3

important a part to play in establishing the new life, that it is not surprising that they are early stirred into activity. Most women feel a sense of fullness and heaviness in quite early weeks. By the end of the eighth week the whole of the brown circle (or areola) round the nipple has become larger and darker in colour, and the tiny oil glands on its perimeter more noticeable. As early as the fourth month a little sticky fluid, known as the colostrum, can sometimes be expressed.

Morning Sickness
Sign number three can be morning sickness, although fortunately about one-third of all mothers-to-be escape it altogether. Another third suffer from waves of nausea in the mornings only; the remaining third are not only actually sick, but may be troubled in this way right through the day. This 'sign' usually commences about the seventh week, and is usually over by the end of three months. Such nausea might spring from other causes than a pregnancy.

Bladder Irritability
Frequent urination occurs often during roughly the same period as morning sickness, passing as the uterus rises out of the pelvis and thus away from the bladder.

Pigmentation
Some mothers are troubled with blotches on face and neck, which have earned the name 'the mask of pregnancy'. Fortunately these disappear after the birth. The sweat glands, too, are generally more active.

Enlarging Abdomen
An actual increase in the size of the abdomen is not likely to be noticeable until pregnancy has been determined in other ways. But even then an enlargement of the abdomen could be associated with some type of ill-health needing investigation.

Massaging and pinching of the skin, rubbing in a little animal fat, will tend to prevent stretch marks appearing, and keep the skin supple. The dark line that may appear from the navel to the pubic arch, will gradually fade after the birth.

The position of the rising womb is, however, diagnostic evidence of definite value and helps to determine the stage of pregnancy reached. Its top reaches the navel by the end of the fifth month. By this time the doctor, with his stethoscope, should be able to count baby's heart-beats, and by then, or a little earlier, the mother will have the joy of feeling life in her womb.

Quickening

Movement, of course, has been going on all the time, but not till the little muscles and joints are well formed are they strong enough to call attention to themselves. The first flutterings may be very faint, and the actual date of 'quickening', as it is called, depends on the amount of fluid the mother is carrying, and her own sensitivity, as well as baby's vigour. Round about the eighteenth to twentieth week, or roughly mid-term, is the most usual date.

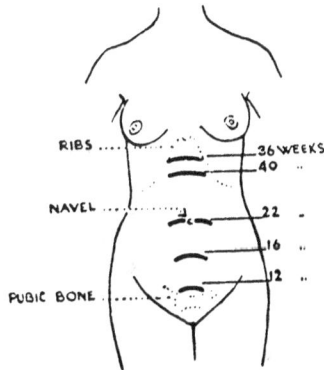

The position of the top of the womb as it rises during pregnancy

Pregnancy Tests

In certain cases, it is desirable for the pregnancy to be confirmed as early as possible. There are various laboratory tests which will give an accurate result in 95 per cent. of all such cases, and nowadays a test of this kind can be taken even as early as 10 days after a missed period. The Family Planning Association run a Laboratory for the purpose at 64, Sloane Street, London, S.W.1, where the cost of the test is 25s.

X-Ray

When a multiple pregnancy is suspected, or where the position of the womb needs watching, an X-ray is helpful and diagnostically final. It is best to postpone this until the twentieth week, to get a really clear picture.

Calculating Dates

The average duration of pregnancy is 266 days or 38 weeks, though variations of from 240 to 300 days can be considered normal. To make a right estimate as to the birth date, take the first day of the

5

last period, count back 3 calendar months and then add on 7 days. Or, if addition is preferred to subtraction, count forward 9 calendar months from the same starting point and again add 7 days.

Just as soon as a pregnancy is suspected, and in any case, after the missing of a second period, a doctor should be consulted, so that plans for ante-natal care and for the confinement can be put in train, and minor troubles corrected early. The doctor will want to read the blood pressure, to measure the pelvis, take the weight and in other ways ensure that all goes as smoothly as possible throughout the waiting-time and that the confinement is well supervised. He will also help to calculate the date of the birth as accurately as possible and will have various checks to help him in this.

A specimen of the mother's blood is usually taken at a first visit in order to test for possible anaemia and to assess her blood grouping. The latter will be of great importance should a transfusion ever be necessary.

The Rh Factor

The majority of folk have a substance in their blood known as the Rh factor, and hence are 'Rh positive'. About 15 per cent lack this substance, and are known as 'Rh negative'. There is nothing for the mother to worry about if she is in this minority group, but it is important to let whoever is caring for her know it, partly to avoid the risk of a wrong admixture of blood, and partly because, in a few cases—fortunately only rarely—some transmission occurs viâ the placenta which affects the blood-cells of the developing infant. Appropriate blood tests in the later stages of pregnancy enable this difficulty, should it occur, to be recognized and treatment instituted.

Those who would like to read a little more on this subject can obtain a threepenny pamphlet entitled 'What Rh Negative is and means' from the Family Doctor, B.M.A., Tavistock Square, W.C.1, postage extra.

FOR FURTHER READING

My Baby's Book, from 'The Woman's Pictorial', The Fleetway House, London, E.C.4., 1s. by post.
Advice to the Expectant Mother (10th edn., 1953), by F. J. Browne. E. and S. Livingstone Ltd., 1s.
Having a Baby (1954), by J. F. Robinson. E. and S. Livingstone, 6s. 6d.

III

DIET FOR
THE EXPECTANT MOTHER

WHEN A BABY is born, he is already nine months old. During those nine months, the change is made from the minutest little speck to a complete living baby, some seven pounds in weight, and some twenty-one inches in length. Never again will the rate of growth of bone and muscle and tissue be so rapid.

The mother's body may be likened to the most marvellous of factories that even the most inventive of minds could conceive. In it millions of tiny cells are busy. Each cell has its own special work. Some make skin, some muscle, some bone, some blood. Others nerves, brain, glands, heart, lungs, stomach, bowels. Still others are set aside for the making of new life some twenty years or so later. A miracle is going on, and the mother's part is to supply the builders through the blood-stream with oxygen and good food material; and to avoid handicapping them by generating poisons from over-fatigue, indigestion, decayed teeth, stuffy rooms or worrying thoughts. The cells can only receive their needed rations and building materials through her blood-stream viâ the cord and the placenta.

In the first months there is little need for the mother to think in terms of eating for two as regards *quantity*, but she must eat for the health of two in regard to *quality*. If the mother-to-be does not take sufficient protein for both, baby, in taking his share, will weaken her and miscarriage may follow. If she does not take sufficient iron for two, baby, in taking his share, may leave her anaemic, depressed and fatigued. If she does not take sufficient calcium for two, baby, in taking his share, may rob her teeth, her hair and even her bones, leaving her run-down and nervous, a prey to toothache, cramp and aches and pains of various kinds.

Protein and fats

The expectant and nursing mother should plan to take dairy products liberally—milk, cheese, eggs and butter or vitaminized margarine; fish at least twice a week, particularly herrings and roes; liver and other offal when obtainable, and other meat, say, three times a week. Well-ground nuts, such as almonds, pea-nuts, walnuts, and hazel nuts, can be eaten with advantage. Some of her protein can be taken in the form of soya, lentils and other pulses.

Raw Food

She must remember every day to include a good proportion of food which has not been subjected to heat (except the natural heat of the sun), for only in this way can she be quite sure of getting the virtues of sunshine into the system, as well as yet unrecognized vitamins, quite apart from those that have been tabulated.

So the expectant mother should take generous servings of salads daily, including celery, watercress, grated carrots, beets and other root vegetables; while raw shredded cabbages and brussel sprouts, etc., are useful additions. She should also take any sun-ripened fruit which may be obtainable, particularly apples, oranges and pears, though all fruits in season, including bananas and sun-dried fruits, are good.

Carbohydrates

Remember that the whole-grain cereals and flours, pure honey and ripe fruits are balanced natural foods, whereas the very refined cereals, sugars and white flour, etc., have lost essential minerals. The home-made wholemeal loaf, using compost-grown and stone-ground flour, is an ideal. This will ensure her ration of vitamin B. Where a good loaf is not available the germ of the wheat in a form such as Bemax or Froment is needed.

Roughly, what is happening is that, first of all the womb and placenta are prepared; then the brain and skeleton of the foetus are developed; then its internal organs and muscles, and finally fat is laid down under the skin and finishing touches put.

Vitamins

Each stage is important, but the need of extra nourishment in the way of minerals, vitamins and proteins in the last nine weeks, and

8

freedom from feverish attacks in the first nine, are especially vital. Vitamin A at the beginning is specially important because it helps to keep the body in good condition and to resist infections. Fish oils are a very good source of vitamin A, but it is also found in milk, cheese, butter, egg yolk, and derived from carrot, green vegetables, kidney and liver.

To take some form of cod-liver oil to ensure vitamins A and D is a wise plan. The mother-to-be can get this, as well as her ration of Government fruit juice, (providing vitamin C), either free or at a cheap rate, from Welfare food distribution centres appointed by the Local Authorities. Should the fresh element be scarce she should take some antiscobutic tablets as an extra source of vitamin C. (See p. 229 for Vitamin table.)

Minerals

Many mothers are a little anaemic so it is wise to ask the doctor if extra iron is needed. Additional calcium is sometimes necessary too when the teeth are poor, or if there is general debility, and the doctor may advise a course of calcium tablets in addition to foods rich in this element.

Foods to eat only in the strictest moderation are cakes, biscuits, white sugar, white flour, twice-cooked dishes, fried foods, preserved and salted foods, condiments and pickles. When the appetite is poor the mother should get out more into the open and try to improve her vitality rather than forcing herself to eat.

Cravings

A strange desire for some special dish should not be rigorously suppressed as it is probably nature's way of making known a deficiency of some particular element. If the mother partakes freely of the pickle, or whatever it may be she longs for, while increasing variety in her menus, the longing will soon lose its importunity.

Fluid

The unborn baby lies in a bed of water, and is composed of 97 per cent of water, so it is important to drink some six to eight glasses of water a day. This is best done in between meals, rather than with them.

Digestion

Thorough mastication, so important to good digestion, is helped or hindered by the state of the teeth, while the latter may be a hiding-place of infective material. To improve the gums, thus nourishing the roots of the teeth, it helps to squeeze them between finger and thumb, really firmly, three or four times a day. Any toothbrush should be fairly soft, so as not to irritate the gums, which may be rather tender. A mouth-wash of salted water (1 teaspoon to 1 pint) is hardening and disinfecting.

After the fifth month, the size of the womb makes it usually better to have five or six smaller meals rather than three larger ones.

If there is a desire to nibble at snacks between meals this may point either to indigestion or to a wrongly-balanced menu and steps to improve matters should be taken.

The father-to-be's co-operation in enjoying a simple, healthful type of meal, keeping cooking to the minimum, will be a service both to his wife and the unborn child.

Raspberry Leaf Tea

Herbalists in many countries consider that a concoction of young raspberry leaves, wild or cultivated, taken during pregnancy has a purifying effect on the blood-stream, and so tones up the uterus that it acts with a vitality which often reduces the times of labour considerably.

Raspberry leaves are obtainable as herbs from which a tea or infusion can be made, or in a blended tablet form, from any herbalist and also from Messrs. Heath and Heather, St. Albans, Herts.; Kerbina Ltd, 177, Vauxhall Bridge Road, London, S.W.1.

FOR FURTHER READING

Nutrition and Health (1953), by Sir R. McCarrison and H. M. Sinclair, 12s. 6d.

Salads for All Seasons, from the London Health Centre, 9, Wigmore Street, London, W.1, postage 6d.

The Mother's Diet, from 'Mother and Home', 32, Southampton Street, London, W.C.2, 2½d. by post.

IV

REST AND RELAXATION

THE EXPECTANT MOTHER is doing a big job, and though she should never consider herself in any way an invalid, all throughout the waiting months she needs extra rest. Early bed with windows wide; short siestas after meals, with the feet and legs above the level of the body, and a longer midday rest on the bed should be the rule whenever possible.

For resting-times to give the maximum refreshment, the mother must be fully relaxed, and this is an art which has been largely lost by this generation. To acquire it early in pregnancy, to practise it daily, and put it into use during the confinement itself will pay big dividends.

Many people believe themselves to be relaxed when this is far from being the case. It is a big help to have someone to act as teacher and guide at first, thus dropping all sense of responsibility. Any tenseness of the mind or emotions makes physical relaxation almost impossible, for mind and body are so closely attuned. Therefore the aim is to thoroughly 'let go', to become drowsy and limp, with every part of the being at rest.

A comfortable position is essential. If sitting, choose a low chair,

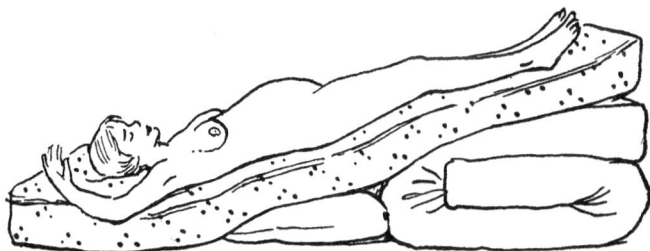

See that hips and feet are raised during rest period

sit well back in it with a small pillow under the head and arms supported on rests. If lying on the back, use a firm mattress and pillow, or a rug on the floor. A pillow under the knees is often helpful too. In later pregnancy, relaxing is best done on the side, with a pillow under one leg, which is drawn well up, and with one arm hanging loosely over the bed, and the other lying comfortably at the back.

Before taking up a posture, tense everywhere, tautening all muscles, stretching, yawning, expanding the ribs. Relaxation best follows strong effort.

Correct breathing is part of the technique to acquire. It does much to steady the nerves, and will be used during labour—deep abdominal breathing during the first stage of labour, and quick chest breathing during the second. Lying flat, with mouth closed, draw in a good breath through the nose, raising the abdominal wall, hold it and let it escape quietly. Repeat several times, and at intervals throughout the day. Chest breathing is done more rapidly and with open mouth.

Mental Relaxation

To help the mind to relax, first 'let go' all the facial muscles, smoothing the forehead, loosening eyelids and brows, letting the cheek and jaw muscles sag. Then think of a really peaceful scene—

quiet moving water, or dark velvet, or a green grassy bank, or a blue lake. Let this image refresh and rest, expelling all the active, worrying thoughts with which the mind is usually full.

In learning muscle relaxation, it is often a good plan initially to take a group at a time. For instance, clench the hand, relax; arch the wrist, relax; tighten the elbow, relax; bend the elbow, relax; tighten the shoulder muscle, relax. Go through a similar proceeding with toes, foot, ankle, knee and hip. See that the solar plexus is relaxed, and deep breathing will help here.

As relaxing proceeds, the body first of all feels very heavy, as if it would fall through the bed; then, as the relaxation gets deeper still, it becomes wonderfully light; the bed seems to rise and cushion it, and there is often a peaceful floating feeling, which ends in falling into a sound sleep.

As the circulation slows down during a drowsy period, getting up again should be done gradually. Take a few deep breaths, stretch well and sit up slowly. Now take some more breaths before putting your feet to the ground; finally, after a pause, stand up.

Mental relaxing can be practiced frequently throughout the day, and when up against any stress or strain will be found to be a useful form of 'counting ten'.

Spiritual relaxation is found in the practise of prayer, and a simple trust in God stays and rests the mind in a wonderful way.

Relaxing during Labour
During labour (see p. 46), as the birth passages open, two sets of opposing muscles are brought into effective play. Their action, entirely involuntary, will progress smoothly, unless the mother, through nervousness or fear, contracts her muscles or holds her body in a tense way. The effect of such tension is to throw a spanner into the works; the muscles of expansion are prevented from doing their work; and less blood reaches the whole area, which tends to make the ensuing contractions both less effective and more painful.

If, however, the mother knows how to let go and keep passive and fear-free throughout each contraction, all will proceed with harmony, and she herself will not get over-tired. Then when the active bearing-down stage is reached, she should aim to relax as soon as each pain passes, conserving her strength, and her peace of mind, in so doing.

13

Rest and Relaxation

Hundreds of mothers who have used this technique—together with postural and toning exercises—are enthusiastic as to the results obtained, making a normal birth a thoroughly satisfying achievement, instead of a dreaded ordeal.

FOR FURTHER READING

A Way to Natural Childbirth (1949), by H. Heardman. E. and S. Livingstone, 7s. 6d.

Release from Nervous Tension, by David Fink. Allen & Unwin, 10s. 6d.

Introduction to Motherhood, 1950, by D. G. Read. Heinemann, 7s. 6d.

The Art of Relaxing, from 'Mother and Home', 32, Southampton Street, London, W.C.2, 2½d. by post.

V

EXERCISE DURING PREGNANCY

WE ALL KNOW the strain that the body feels after some unusual exercise, and the sense of stiffness which follows. Now in giving birth to a baby all the joints, ligaments and muscles will be called into strenuous and unaccustomed play, but especially those of the spine and pelvic area. It is only common sense to prepare these for their task well in advance.

Ideally the mother-to-be will join a physiotherapy class in her neighbourhood. If one does not exist there are some inexpensive illustrated books available, describing a series of exercises which can easily be put into practice at home (see p. 18).

In such exercise there is a threefold aim: one, to strengthen all the muscles which will be used at the birth: two, to make all joints, ligaments and muscles flexible, so that good expansion is possible: three, to avoid sluggishness and congestion of the pelvic area,—very likely to occur as the uterus becomes heavier and takes up more room.

Many domestic routines can be readily adapted to this threefold end. For widening the pelvic floor, for instance, any squatting movement helps. Incidentally, do have a largish, firm stool or box in the lavatory for your feet; and if, in addition, a stout chair is placed in front of the foot support, so that you can grasp its back, you will soon find constipation a thing of the past. The contact of the thighs with the abdominal wall exerts a pressure on the bowel, while grasping with the hands and pressing with the feet enables the muscles to act strongly.

Then, for the spine, polishing, dusting, bed-making, can all help to keep it flexible. In polishing the floor, etc., on hands and knees not only is the spine exercised but also, as the weight of the womb is taken on the front of the pelvis, a tendency to backache is relieved and the front muscles are strengthened. A position on one knee,

15

with the body following the duster's direction, up and down and round about, is also excellent.

Going upstairs abdominal tone can be increased by an erect posture and by doing a little conscious knee-raising. Even when sitting some rocking exercise which will help to keep the pelvic organs

Exercises during pregnancy

1. (A) Crouching, knees apart—a useful position to adopt frequently. (B) Sitting with rounded back. Clasp knees and draw them as widely apart as possible.
2. Rounding and hollowing back while on all fours. (A) Start with spine straight; then (B) arch lower back bending head forwards and downwards. Next relax spine to form a deep hollow.
3. Hold on to something firm for balance. (A) Sit on heels, knees apart; close knees and lower heels. (B) Raise heels, part knees, hollowing back. (C) Rise on tip-toe, tightening muscles of buttocks and knees. Hold. Relax, lowering body, with pelvic area as wide as possible.
4. (A and B) Polishing on hands and knees, and using dust-pan in crouching position, strengthens muscles, and improves the circulation of the pelvic area.

supple can be done. Sit well forward, the feet and knees well apart, and rock forward, hollowing the back and pressing the knees outwards with the hands, and then rock backwards, rounding the back and allowing the thighs to relax. An old-fashioned rocking-chair makes an excellent seat during the waiting months.

Good posture is important right through the day. It aids the circulation, prevents sagging of the organs, and unconsciously improves morale. When standing, care must be taken not to stoop forward as if trying to disguise the pregnancy; nor to lean backwards, developing an ugly waddling stance, and weakening the back. Instead, imagine a plumb line passing from the head through the body, which ends between the balls of the feet. These should point straight forward, and not be turned outwards at all. The head should be held erect, as if carrying a basket, neither tilting backwards nor forwards. Always to sit, walk and stand 'tall', and yet be completely free from tenseness is the ideal.

Good breathing and good air are important, not only to ensure adequate oxygen for the unborn child, but in order to strengthen the nervous system, so try to avoid stuffy places. Breathing should come from the diaphragm rather than the chest and should help to expand the ribs. Breathe in very gently through the nose, and out, with a prolonged expiration, to get rid of all the stale air at the base of the lungs. (See also p. 12.)

Shoes
To enjoy getting out of doors every day, rain or fine, well-shod feet are essential, choosing footwear, which give protection, comfort and support. A wide one-inch heel suits many mothers; others find the wedge-heel better. High heels place a strain on the calf muscles and foot arches, as well as tilting the pelvis, leading to risk of falls, as the balance shifts with the enlarging womb.

Carrying Weights
Few mothers can get through a pregnancy without having both to pick up and to carry weights of various kinds. It is worth then taking trouble to plan so that there is a minimum strain involved.

First tenseness should be avoided, particularly of arm and shoulder muscles and spine. Next the knee, rather than hip joints, should be used, and the back must not be kept straight and stiff. With one foot in front of the other, squat down as near to the weight to be lifted as possible and then rise smoothly. If picking up a child the hip can be used to support him. Do not lean backwards when carrying a weight, as this compresses the spine and prevents easy breathing.

If carrying, say, a heavy tray, especially upstairs, to lean just very slightly forward and to hold the tray near the body, elbows loose is best. When things must be lifted down from a height, a stool or firm step-ladder should be used when possible, and hollowing the back avoided.

Activities

Good exercise includes brisk walking; hill-climbing, if enjoyed; swimming in shallow water, providing there is no chilling; gardening; and housework with open windows. The right companionship naturally adds much to the enjoyment of any activity, so, while to be out in the sunshine is of greater value than to be out after dark, an evening walk when the husband is home will help to ensure sound sleep, and is a good ending to the day.

Mothers-to-be sometimes wonder whether it is safe to follow strenuous forms of exercise, which they normally enjoy. Much depends on their athletic fitness and general health. Activities to avoid are those which include jolting and jerking movement; sports in which there is a risk of falling; and work which necessitates stretching above the head.

The ordinary movements connected with running, swimming, bending, jumping, to which the individual is accustomed, are not likely to affect matters in the least; but the time will come when, automatically, they will become more laborious, and the mother will find her life becomes more sedate quite naturally. A temptation to overtax the strength should be resisted. Nowadays it is fashionable to be 'fit'; the young wife hates to be a 'spoil sport', and she will cheerfully and gallantly undertake many a venture or jaunt which would have been 'nothing' to her in the old days, and it is here where the discerning husband can be such a help, arranging matters so that a margin of vitality is left untapped, and the reaction from the day's exercise is a healthy one.

FOR FURTHER READING

Introduction to Motherhood, 1950, by G. D. Read. Heinemann, 7s. 6d.
Training for Childbirth, by Minnie Randell. Churchill, 10s. 6d.
Fearless Childbirth, by Minnie Randell. Churchill, 3s. 6d.
Relaxation and Exercises for Natural Childbirth, by Helen Heardman.
    Livingstone Press, 9d.
Exercises before Childbirth, by K. Vaughan. Faber & Faber, 6s.

VI

PREPARATION
FOR BREAST-FEEDING

BREAST-FEEDING IS an experience few mothers would wish to miss
and probably in 95 out of 100 cases there is no need for them to do
so. But it does take some intelligent preparatory planning if all is to
go as smoothly as possible.

Most mothers have happy associations with the whole idea and
rejoice in the thought of being able to nourish their own child in
the early helpless days. Some, unfortunately, consciously or unconsciously have unpleasant ones, and if this is so they should try and
sort out their ideas well in advance, to avoid emotional conflicts
which might interfere with the natural completion of the reproductive cycle.

At a first ante-natal interview the doctor will probably examine
the nipples for, from a physical point of view, it is largely on their
efficiency that success depends.

Preparing the Nipples

It is not always clearly understood that a baby's sucking action
affects the dark disc at its base even more than the tender nipple
itself. This is—or should be—drawn right to the back of the
mouth, so that the pressure of the baby's lips may fall on a
tougher region, and one under which cisterns of milk have collected. Pressure, here too, contracts underlying muscle, and causes
the nipple to stand out well. Supposing the nipple is so short that
baby cannot get it far enough back; supposing he can't champ on
the dark areola but only on the sensitive nipple tip, thus leading to
soreness and cracks. How can you be sure in advance?

A simple dress rehearsal early in pregnancy will make this plain.
Support the left breast with the left hand, and with finger and
thumb of the right hand—to represent baby's jaws—press on the

19

base of the nipple and note what happens. If the nipple slides forward, well and good. If it tends to shrink back or retract, then you will have to set to work to improve it, if you are to breast-feed successfully.

A practical way of doing this is to apply a gentle, continuous suction by means of glass or plastic shells (the Woolwich), which are obtainable through many chemists, or from John Bell & Croyden, Ltd. of Wigmore Street, W.1. These are far more effective than the occasional rolling and forming, or occasional use of a breast-pump, which is their alternative.

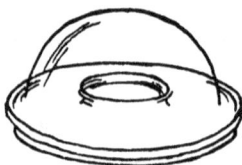

Apart from the prominence of the nipple, the question of easy flow must be considered. Though the majority of nipples have a number of openings, it is possible that they may get blocked. Colostrum, a sticky secretion, is formed from the fifth month, while as pregnancy advances cell layers are shed and this debris passes through the milk ducts, leading towards the nipple. Such secretion should be washed off daily and the nipples dried with good friction.

Breast shield

Expressing by Hand

The ducts may also get blocked after birth when the milk comes in with a rush, as it usually does on the third day. To be able to relieve the breasts by hand-expression is an art the mother should acquire well before the baby's birth. During the last six weeks, therefore, she should express just a little of the fluid to be found in the breasts twice a day. Not only will this technique keep the ducts clear but, should the breasts begin to feel heavy following the birth, the mother will know how to give herself immediate relief without waiting for a busy nurse to come and instruct her. To express, first massage the breasts gently by stroking like the spokes of a wheel towards the nipple with the palm of the hand. Then, supporting one breast with the opposite hand, with thumb and first finger, press rhythmically on the dark disc. The aim is to exert pressure over the whole milk-collecting area, and not just to pull at the nipple. Some mothers find it wise to express when in a warm bath, or after sponging with warm water, as a relaxed breast is softer and more yielding.

While a small thin breast may be quite as active in manufacturing milk as a large one, yet good development of the breasts, with an increase in size over the pre-pregnant state is to be expected.

To stir the milk glands into activity, in some cases it may be wise to sponge the breasts with alternate hot and cold water, or with cold water only, promoting a flow of blood to the underlying tissues. Exposure to sun and air, too, has a tonic affect.

Brassières

The breasts should not be allowed to carry their own weight, but in applying a well-fitting brassière care must be taken to see that there is no constriction over the nipple area. There are special maternity and nursing brassières on the market, some of which can be made to measure, or the mother may evolve her own simple one, especially for night wear.

The nipple must not be allowed to get sodden at any time; and to nourish and maintain elasticity it is often a good plan to rub in a little cream with a lanoline base and to give light friction with a clean bath towel when washing.

With a healthy, well-developed mother, preparation of this kind is probably only needed in the last 6 weeks of pregnancy, but if things are not quite so normal, measures of this kind should start just as soon as pregnancy is established.

FOR FURTHER READING

The Nursing Couple, by Dr. Merell Middlemore. Hamish Hamilton, 7s. 6d.

Breast Feeding, by F. Charlotte Naish. Oxford Medical Publications, 7s. 6d.

Breast Feeding, by Winifred Coppard. N.A.M.H., 39 Queen Anne Street, London, W.1., 1s. 3d.

Early Failure of Breast Feeding, by Dr. H. K. Waller. H. K. Lewis, Ltd., 1s.

VII

MATERNITY WEAR

MANY MOTHERS CANNOT afford much in the way of new clothes for
the waiting months, but every woman will wish to be so dressed that
she feels happy in going out and about, comfortable, and free from
all constriction.

A mother-to-be will find that she keeps warmer than usual and
is inclined to perspire, so a free circulation of air is important for
her health, and an open-mesh garment should be worn next to the
skin. An Aertex or sea-island cotton cellular vest, easy to wash, is
practical; if wool is preferred it should be loosely woven.

The breasts need continuous support but without any compres-
sion. They will be getting heavier so the brassière worn should have
a good depth, be an uplift type and be expandable. Straps should
be wide over the shoulders and preferably fork before they fasten.
A good nursing brassière is usually suitable for the waiting months
too, and thus saves expense.

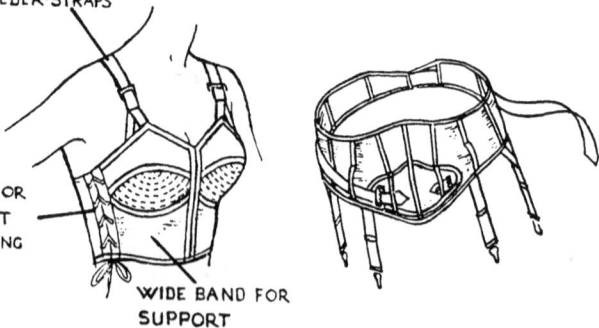

WIDE ADJUSTABLE
SHOULDER-STRAPS

SIDE , OR
FRONT
OPENING

WIDE BAND FOR
SUPPORT

As designed by Dr. Grantly Read.

Maternity belts, if worn, should not be rigid at any point. The

22

muscle fibres of the abdomen need plenty of practice in relaxing and contracting and a strong abdominal wall is really the best corset! For warmth in winter, for suspender attachments, and for taking the weight of the womb in the last three months, some type of girdle is, however, generally required, while those who usually wear corsets will be wise to change to a maternity one from the fourth month.

The National Association of Maternity and Child Welfare Centres, 5 Tavistock Place, W.C.1, supply an inexpensive and practical belt which is 18s. 3d. by post.

Directions for Home Made Maternity Belts

First Method. For two binders buy 2½ yards of strong huckaback towelling, 2 yards of 1-in. wide webbing, or strong tape, and some strong safety-pins. Fold the towelling length-wise about 4 in. deep, lie flat on the bed, and draw the towelling round the body, well over the hips, the folded part at the bottom. The lowest part should be kept quite tight, leaving it looser as the waistline is approached. Safety-pins are the most sensible fastenings. Sew or pin 2 yards of webbing to the back of the binder and pass this over the shoulders, across the breast, and attach to the front. Two sets of stocking suspenders may be attached to the lower edge, one on the hips and one towards the middle front.

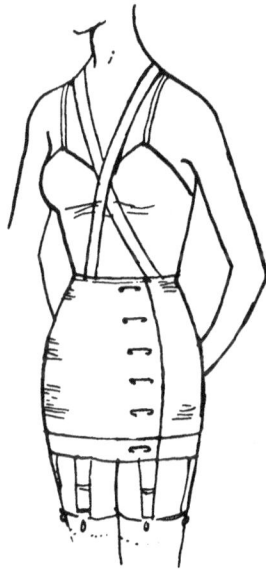

Second Method: The adaptation of the 'many-tailed' bandage will form a convenient and comfortable maternity belt. It should be made of domette, flannel, or Aertex, and the material chosen should measure 54 in. long by 10–12 in. wide. An untorn portion of 10 in. should be left in the centre (back) and the remainder split into eight 'tails', four on each side. Length of shoulder straps 32–36 in.; width 2½ in.

Adjust the 'tails' to suit the figure; they should not pass round the body in a circle, but be directed obliquely downwards, so as to form a 'sling'. First cross the top pair in the middle line of the body and safety-pin, then cross the other 'tails' in succession, securing each 'tail' to the one above. The fourth pair should be passed well below the abdomen so as to form the 'floor' of the sling, and then carried firmly upwards and outwards and fastened at the side. The main point is to apply it correctly so that the weight is slung from the shoulders and all downward pressure avoided.

Cami-knickers seem an ideal second layer as there is no elastic round the waist, and support is from the shoulders and not from the hips. If knickers are worn, loops of tape can be attached to the top edges so that they can be buttoned to vest or bodice. Divide the elastic; sew a button on one end and attach an extra piece of elastic with three or four buttonholes to the other, so that extra width is quickly arranged.

With underwear and night wear it is a good plan to undo the front shoulder-straps and to provide buttons and loops to simplify breast-feeding later on.

Present-day fashions of swagger coats, separates, boleros, duffle coat, and so on are kind to the expectant mother, who has quite a variety of styles to choose from. For home wear some sort of smock and wrap-over skirt is practical. Skirts can be attached to a light bodice with tucks in front to let down when the front hem rises, or worn with light braces. Horizontal zips are incorporated in the belts of some ready-made skirts. Pinafore frocks with adjustable straps on the shoulders are also useful. With frocks, inverted pleats at the sides which go right up under the arm are good, for development is not only at the waistline! Such frocks can be readily reconditioned after a birth as they do not lose their shape. For evening wear, the apron-drape is concealing and attractive; a stole or cape to give importance to the shoulders will help to give balance to the figure.

Plain materials are really better than patterned, and colours should not be too bright, or light, as these draw attention to the figure. For outdoor wear, quite dark materials are best; a light blouse or other top part, is, however, sensible. Swagger or tent coats, short box-coats, or capes can all be worn successfully. An important collar is always a help. Both Bestway and Weldon's maternity patterns are good.

Shoes must be really comfortable and yet give support to the foot. The more active the mother the better, so happy feet are important, while with the changing balance of the body a firm wide base is essential. A cuban, or one inch wide heel is usually best unless a still lower heel suits the individual mother. The inner curve of the shoes should allow free play to the big toe, so that this grips the ground, and one with a fastening to prevent the foot slipping in the shoe, is better than the court type.

VIII

BABY'S LAYETTE

IN PLANNING BABY's clothing we must remember that its real purpose is to conserve the heat manufactured by the body, not actually to make heat. Non-porous clothing, or too many layers of clothing, interfere with the skin's functions and prevent baby's heat-regulating mechanisms acquiring stability. Equally if *all* the clothing were porous, body heat would be dissipated too readily.

The garment worn next the skin is naturally of the first importance. It must be soft as the skin is sensitive; elastic as baby is growing fast; and porous so that body vapours given off are allowed to pass through its mesh, and not held next to the skin.

The long-sleeved vest should be knitted in rib of the softest possible yarn—silk-wool or other mixture is best. If pure wool is used, it is usually wise to make slips of soft butter muslin or gauze, or cellular cotton for baby to wear underneath, for pure wool may make the skin too active and prove irritating, while in warm days it will be too heating. Make the vests about 12 in. long, sleeve 6 in. under arm seam; though this may mean that they need turning back for the first weeks, the mother will soon be glad of her foresight. Reinforce with tape in front so that the vests can be pinned to the napkin without the risk of holes. Directions for knitted vests can be obtained from the Bestway Pattern Department, Amalgamated Press, Bear Alley, E.C.4—leaflet No. 1988, price 4d. plus 2d. postage.

Binders are neither necessary nor desirable. The use of a crêpe

26

bandage 3½ in. wide, which can be cut into three lengths, washing them in turn, is sufficient to hold the cord dressing in place, if one is used, until the naval is healed. Body belts get into uncomfy rucks when loose and constrict the abdominal walls, interfering with the development of the muscles and with the digestive process when tight.

Napkins

Absorbent muslin napkins are particularly comfortable to the skin and very easy to launder, drying quickly. They should be 30 in. square. Towelling napkins will also be needed as baby grows. These should not be larger than 23 in. square, or they will be too heavy and bulky. If making napkins, use a double thickness of butter muslin and boil before use. Various forms of destructible napkins are now on the market, very helpful when travelling, or when nappy washing is a bugbear. Nappy Washing Services exist in some areas and can be a boon.

The petticoat, if worn, should be a simple princess style, about 19 in. long—of flannel, Viyella, Clydella, Daflowna, etc. if worn for warmth; or in cambric if needed under a summer frock.

Frocks should just come below the toes, no more—22–23 in. is a practical first length; and nightgowns 25–26 in. in length. If you favour the set-in sleeve, have large armholes, for any tightness here would soon cause chafing. A raglan or magyar style is really to be preferred. The sleeves should be the same width all the way down and not be set into a cuff. Baby will not oblige you by pushing his

little arms into them; you will have to slip your own hand down each sleeve to find the little wandering fist and gently draw it through, and this is not easy with a narrow opening. Draw-ribbons will gather the sleeve in prettily and cosily for you, ensuring a fit which keeps pace with baby's growth. The round yoke, or the pin tucks or gathers, to control the fullness, can be embroidered to the mother's desire, but should always do up with running ribbons. In this way cold draughts cannot get down the neck, and the garment worn when baby was a day old can often remain in commission right until his second birthday.

Baby has little neck at first. Remember this if you are tempted to finish the neck-hem with lace. If you want lace-trimmed frocks apply the lace *below* the neck-hem, letting it lie flat.

At night a long-sleeved vest and warm flannel nightgown should be worn. A raglan-sleeve jacket gives extra warmth when needed.

Four of each article is a usual number to provide, but if night-gowns are going to give yeoman service, an extra one or two is an advantage.

Bootees

The tiny feet must be kept warm, and bootees should be provided, preferably with a long leg part to reach just above the knee, except in the summer. To knit each with a definite left and right is an ideal —even slight pressure may spoil perfect foot development. Cold feet are a fruitful cause of wakefulness and colic, but damp, over-warm feet can lead to chest trouble, so in warm weather baby is better with his feet uncovered. A great deal of perspiration passes from feet and hands, thus neither socks or gloves should be worn unnecessarily. In this, as in all else, the mother must be guided by the little one's reactions and the day's temperature.

To keep little hands warm in cold weather loose flannel bags tied lightly above the elbow are suitable.

Headgear

Baby should not usually wear a bonnet. If he wears one out-of-doors, he will miss it and be liable to catch cold in passages and cold rooms. It is as well, however, to provide a bonnet for special occasions, lining it with silk or muslin to prevent irritation of the scalp.

Pilches will be needed to keep baby tidy when out of the cot; to provide extra warmth in cold weather; and to protect other clothes. These are best of flannel, or they can be knitted; they should button to vest or bodice rather than being held up by elastic. Plastic or nylon knickers can be worn at times if well ventilated.

For pram wear, overall leggings, which come right up to the waist are ideal. They should be sufficiently roomy to allow for napkins, and there must, of course, be no pull on the foot. Pram coats with raglan sleeves are best, as these slip on easily over other garments. They should be double-breasted, fit snugly at the throat, and be knitted in a firm tension to make a strong close weave.

A carrying shawl will be needed for out-of-doors; this should be at least $1\frac{1}{2}$ yards square. Two soft baby shawls for use indoors could be about a yard square. Small Shetland shawls are convenient, but should be of a good quality to stand up to wear and give warmth. Avoid too much pattern or open mesh work in which baby may entangle his fingers.

All Knitted Layette

Some mothers prefer to dress their babies in an all-knitted layette —vest, jersey, knickers and pull-overs. This is an economical plan, but the knitting needs to be even and firm, and the laundering painstaking, if the woollies are not to lose their shape. As you cannot put tucks or pleats into knitted wear, choose patterns which enable you to knit on further rows as baby grows. Except in warm weather a light flannel bodice under the jersey is advisable when baby spends more time out of shawls and blankets.

Materials

Some mothers like to make baby's layette in the sunshine colour of a pale yet bright yellow; some feel a blue (for a boy) or pinky shade gives baby an extra charm; others like white for that first stage of innocence, adding a touch of colour here and there.

It is not an economy to buy cheap materials for the layette as everything has to be washed so frequently. Choose pre-shrunken materials when you can, or shrink them yourself before making up. Remember that animal products such as wool and real silk are always warmer than vegetable ones such as cotton and rayon; that there is no wool in either winceyette or flannelette, and also that no

inflammable materials should be used near a baby. For summer-
time and for best wear, silks, muslins or cotton crêpe can be worn
as wished. In all your planning, think more of your little one's
health and comfort than of your pride in his appearance. He will
look charming in the simplest outfit.

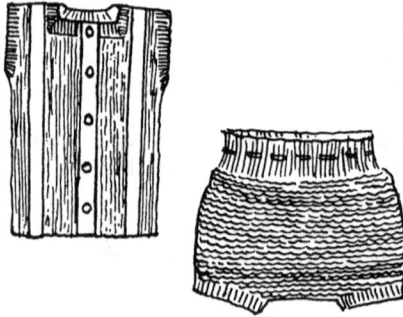

GOOD LAYETTE PATTERNS

Bestway Pattern No. C.315, including raglan frock and magyar
nightgown, petticoat, matinee jacket and little bodice and pilch.
2s. Home, 2s. 3d. Overseas. (Pattern Department, 21, Whitefriars
Street, London, E.C.4.)

Weldon's Layette Pattern 9029, with a tucked magyar frock,
gathered magyar nightgown, scalloped matinee jacket, princess petticoat. 2s. (Weldons Ltd., 30–32, Southampton Street, Strand, London,
W.C.2.)

FOR FURTHER READING

Baby's First Knitted Layette, 'Mother and Home', 32, Southampton
Street, London, W.C.2, 4d., plus postage.
Baby's Second Woollies, from 'Mother and Home', 32, Southampton
Street, London, W.C.2, 4d., plus postage.

IX

THE NURSERY
AND ITS EQUIPMENT

It is rarely feasible nowadays to give baby a day and a night nursery, but if possible he should have an airy and sunny room in which to sleep and later to play. Windows on different walls provide excellent cross-ventilation, catch the morning or afternoon sun, and make it easy to keep an open window when the wind veers.

Nursery walls should be washable—paint is good as it is easy to clean, especially for the lower part of the room, which little fingers will soon be touching. Distemper, or washable wallpaper, can be used higher up if expense must be considered. Ceilings should be of some soft shade, as white is too dazzling for baby's eyes. A dado of dark paint, to be used later as a blackboard, may be a useful idea.

The windows should be fitted with vertical safety-bars straight away, and these should be not further than 6 in. apart. Curtains should be short, light and washable; and as it should be possible to darken the room, to exclude strong sunlight, when necessary, if outside blinds, or slatted Venetian blinds can be provided it is good.

The floor—on which in a few months baby will be crawling—should be covered with a material warm to the feel and easy to clean. Cork carpeting, or rubber, are excellent. One or two washable rugs are a cheerful and decorative extra.

Heating

Aim to have heating which can be quickly turned off and on, and which does not make dust and dirt; but it is not wise to block up an open fireplace. If using electricity, get an expert to vet and protect all the fittings; and use a good guard, sufficiently far from the element not to get over-hot. If an open fire is used, in this or any other room in the house, see that the fireguard has a covered top, and can be, and is, firmly fixed.

31

Baby's special furniture will include cradle, bath, screen and basket. Mother will need a low chair without arms for bathing him, while a visitor's chair and small table will be useful. Later he will

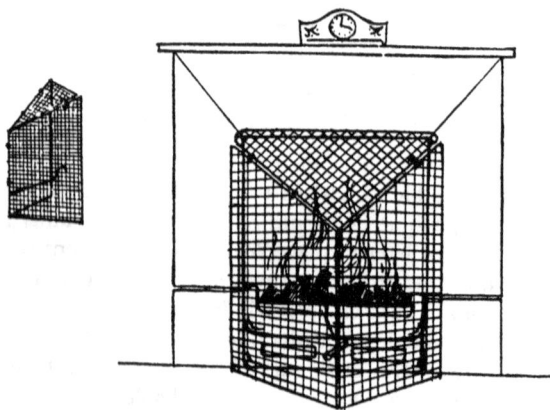

need crib, play-pen, small wardrobe for hanging clothes, low chair and table for himself, toy cupboard and shelves. A handy-man could make many of these and they could be enamelled in soft colours.

Baby's Bed

Among the many types of cradle available, a simple wicker one on a stand is hard to beat. It is light, portable and airy. Closed sides, or layers of trimming, are as stuffy as the bed-hangings beloved of the Victorians. They also catch and hold germ-laden dust.

A fold of voile, or muslin or silk at the cot-head makes a soft decoration, breaks a draught here and is easily washed. This is all that is necessary in the way of trimming, and if baby's bed is made up correctly the open undraped sides will be all to the good.

A firm mattress is essential from the earliest days, so that there will be no sagging of the spine. A chaff overlay makes a cool, comfortable and hygienic nest for baby very inexpensively, while protecting the under mattress. To make, obtain three yards of calico, or similar strong material, and a bushel of bedding chaff from a corn merchant. Go over this to break up any prickly pieces, and bake in a tin in the oven for about an hour. Make two cases the same length and width as the mattress, half-fill with chaff, shaking evenly through. A thin chaff pillow can also be used if wished, though this is not essential. Should any of the chaff become soiled, it is readily renewable.

If no overlay is used, the mattress must be protected by a washable cover of which one side can be rubber, but it is better to use a separate waterproof draw-sheet, which does not come higher than the shoulders. Strips of sheeting, stitched to this, will help to hold it tautly in place.

To make up baby's cradle, (a) lay a fluffy blanket, size 70 in. by 44 in., on the floor of the cradle, before putting in mattress and

Making up the cot

33

overlay. (*b*) Cover the latter with an old piece of blanket, or winceyette or flannelette. Then across the middle part put a piece of rubber sheeting about 21 in. by 12 in. (*c*) Cover this with a drawsheet of flannel, or use a Harrington cot pad. Put a soft pillow-slip in place. Now a little 'nest' is made with the hand and baby laid down. First the nestling shawl is arranged cosily over him, and then each side of the enveloping blanket is brought across in turn, securing at one side with a safety-pin if wished. (*d*) The foot part of the blanket is folded envelope-wise so that, to all intents and purposes, baby is in a cosy sleeping-bag. In cold weather an extra blanket will be needed—a cellular one is warm and light. A light porous cover, of a cellular mesh, which can be prettily embroidered if wished, can go over all.

Though sheets are not a necessity, many mothers like to provide them. They keep the blankets fresh, prevent baby swallowing fluff, and are soft to the feel. Aertex sheets seem ideal, but those of winceyette may be used. There is also a cotton 'glove sheet' which fits tautly over the mattress, holding the draw sheet snugly in place.

Baby's Bath

If baby is to use his bath for some months it should be deep enough

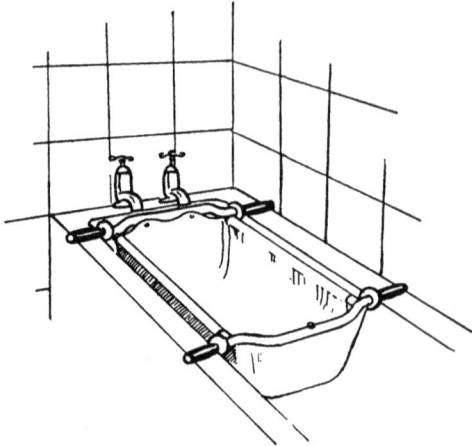

to enable him to splash around and take exercise as he grows. It should also be on a stand, or chairs, to save his mother's back. The

'Poppet' folding bath, which fits on to the top of a big bath, so that it can be filled from the taps and easily emptied is a recent innovation well worth considering. It is made of light rust-proof steel and white plastic and folds up conveniently. A folding rubber bath, with a tap underneath, is a further alternative.

A screen has many uses in a nursery. A small light one, made by covering a two-fold clothes-horse with chintz or cretonne can be

The nursery equipped

used to break a draught, or shield the eyes from glare, without interfering with the free movement of air round the cradle. In a largish room, where a cosy corner is needed, a three-fold screen will be an asset. Remove the lower bars of a three-fold clothes-horse to within four inches of the ground, and cover with pretty, close-woven material.

Basket

It is a great help if all baby's toilet accessories are kept together in one place, and a wicker basket, or clean, lined box can be used for the purpose, standing this ideally on a trolley. A protective cover, weighted with beads, or with elastic run round the edges, will be

35

needed if there is no lid. If a small chest-of-drawers can be provided for baby it will last him many years, but any clean drawer or box will do to store his clothes.

Baby Scales
To be able to weigh baby in the home is often a real convenience, but scales are very expensive. Kitchen scales can be fitted with a special baby basket, or very good scales can be hired by the month (see p. 74.) Clock-faced scales, or those with a spring balance, are not accurate enough to be of much value, as baby is usually on the move.

THE PRAM

Though a perambulator is not an essential at first, it is a convenience, both as an out-of-door bed and as a mode of transport.

Points to consider when choosing a pram are size—both in relation to baby's growth and your own storage accommodation; convertibility, in case you may want to use it for two; balance, to ensure that it does not tip easily, when baby is older and heavier and inclined to bounce about in it; springs, to reduce shock and strain; brakes, to ensure safety; and good materials that will stand up to all sorts of weather.

If possible discuss these points with an understanding salesman, or study catalogues carefully, before making a purchase. Do not be guided by appearance only, and do test to make sure that the handles are a convenient height. Large wheels make for easy travelling, and 16 in. diameter in front and 18 in. at the back are useful sizes, with a carriage body length of 36 in. The safety-strap should have its pull from within the wheel base, i.e. the attachment should not be fastened too near the hood end.

Baby should not lie too low in the pram, so a mattress should be used over the leather cushions and this will also give extra comfort. The hood, while essential on occasions, should not be raised unnecessarily, for under it the air soon becomes stale and stuffy. To keep the hood up when the pram is not in use, and down when it is, is a good working generalization. To half raise the hood to break a cold wind is, however, often advisable. Leather aprons should only be used when it is actually raining.

If it can be afforded, a canopy,—best lined with green—should be obtained to use in bright weather when natural shade is not available. Its sides should not be too deep, or too much air will be cut off.

Care of pram

To keep a pram in good order, use a little furniture cream for coach-built prams, or car polish such as, Autobrite, for metal-sided one. Chrome fittings will be preserved by using an oily rag over them frequently, and a drop of oil should be used regularly for less accessible parts, nuts and screws. To oil the inside of the mud-guards, prevents rust and mud-caking. Leather aprons can be washed with mild soap and warm water, rinsed and dried.

X

THINGS AMISS

PREGNANCY IS A wonderful time for building positive good health, for the glandular activity with which it is associated makes it easier than usual to put right anything that may be amiss.

On these grounds alone, it is only common sense to tackle any minor ailments that crop up during the waiting-period, and not just to grin and bear them as 'something to be expected'.

Studies of the ailments of pregnancy carried out by the People's League of Health, and by certain hospitals, have demonstrated most clearly that by proper ante-natal care, proper instruction of the mother, and a proper diet, still-births and premature births can be markedly reduced in number; for difficulties which used to be considered almost inevitable clear like magic when tackled aright.

One group of such divergencies from full health is concerned with the *digestion*—constipation, heartburn, flatulence, disturbed sleep, and, in some cases, morning sickness. The chapter on diet, (p. 7) will give pointers in regard to the vital foods needed by the body to prevent deficiencies, and to avoid over-acidity.

Constipation may be troublesome at times; remember to adopt the squatting attitude for stool, so that the abdominal muscles are not handicapped but strengthened (see page 15). Be sure to take enough fluid and roughage. Should a laxative ever be needed, choose one that is non-habit forming, discontinuing it as soon as possible, but gradually. Dried fruits soaked over-night with brown sugar and lemon juice, are laxative in effect. The juice can be taken on waking and the fruit at the breakfast meal, combined with All-Bran, or wheat germ. Do remember to take your apple a day.

Heartburn. To avoid heartburn, adopt a good stance, for slumping compresses the digestive organs. For acidity try chewing a few almonds to a cream in the mouth occasionally, or taking a charcoal biscuit, or a few sips of ginger ale. Anti-acid powders and pills are on the market, and can be used occasionally, but try to deal with basic causes rather than relying on these chemical reliefs. Meat, fish or egg, all acid-forming foods, should be balanced with a sufficiency of greens and salads, as these are alkaline. Remember cold foods tend to depress the activity of the acid-making glands; fatty stews, and soups, should be avoided.

For flatulence, much the same rules apply. Avoid any foods such as cauliflower and cabbage if you find them 'windy'. Chew and chew your food so that the saliva starts its digestion before it goes on to the stomach. Try not to get into the habit of seeking to relieve symptoms with soda bicarb, as in any excess this will do harm. Do not seek to hold the wind back but let it come away.

For morning sickness, it is a good plan to reduce all fat in the diet, as well as cutting out any food that experience has shown leads to digestive discomfort. Take your meals as dry as possible, but drink fluid an hour before them. Put away the frying-pan; give up the white loaf and take less refined sugar. Have a sweetened fruit drink and a dry biscuit by your bedside, and sip and nibble in the morning before raising your head from the pillow. To get up very slowly, sitting on the bed awhile, or putting the head down low, helps to stabilize the circulation; and in dressing see that your clothing is loose everywhere.

Varicose veins

Another set of possible discomforts is associated with the *circulation* more than with the digestion—such things as varicose veins, piles, cramp, etc. They are in part due to pressure from the enlarging uterus, affecting veins, lymphatics and nerves. To keep the blood circulating actively by simple limbering exercise, brisk walking and friction of the skin, will be helpful. See, too, that some of the weight is taken off the pelvic veins by wearing a simple sling-belt as the womb gets heavier. Drain the legs well two or three times a day; to do this you can lie half-way down the bed, and rest the feet against the wall at its head. Or double a mattress and lie on an incline on this; or arrange a low plank against a sofa; or build up the foot of the bed on books or blocks by about 12 in. In some cases special elastic stockings, or bandages, may have to be worn.

The mother-to-be will be wise to avoid standing when sitting will do, and, when sitting, to have the feet well raised, or to squat on the floor tailor-fashion. Employment which involves much standing should be given up at least two months before the birth.

Cramp can often be relieved by a little simple rubbing and massage and stretching of the affected area; hot and cold compresses will be needed in more serious cases. If it follows perspiration, a salt drink is indicated.

Piles are best prevented by keeping the stools soft and avoiding straining at stool. Witch-hazel lotion or cream, or Fissan anal ointment is helpful in dealing with them. If they are painful and protruding, cold applications will benumb them and reduce their size.

Anaemia. A tendency to anaemia, very common during pregnancy, and leading to a state of fatigue, can be combatted by eating more of the foods containing iron, and, if necessary, taking iron medicinally.

Sleeplessness is another trying symptom which tends to depress the vitality. See that the mattress is really comfortable and sleep as low as possible, except towards the last weeks when an extra pillow is often helpful. Have a hot-water bottle and use a small pillow under the waist to give support where specially needed. Try and go for a 'constitutional' before turning in and sleep with windows wide open. The better you can relax in bed the sooner sleep will come; a warm bath helps. Try to view the day's happenings in terms of confidence and peace, as far as you can, refusing negative, worrying thoughts as they crowd in on you. Remember with gratitude that you are in partnership with the Creator of all men; there is no need to carry your burdens single-handed.

The kidneys are called on to throw off waste products of mother and child and this extra work will show up any weak spot in them. Part of good ante-natal care is to have the urine tested regularly. If it tends to become scanty or abnormal in any way, this must at once be reported; also puffiness of hands, eyelids, or swelling of ankles and feet.

The blood pressure must also be taken for it will reveal incipient toxaemia. Blurred vision, headaches, pain under the breast-bone, etc., should be reported to a doctor and are a signal of the need to increase elimination of poisons from the blood-stream. In such a case salt should be cut right out of the diet as far as possible, and rest in bed under expert supervision will almost certainly be needed.

A too-rapid gain in weight not only leads to discomfort and fatigue, but is usually a sign that all is not well, so regular weighing is important.

Miscarriage

If a miscarriage should occur, it will do so in the large majority of cases before the 12th week, though the term is usually applied to any interruption of pregnancy which occurs before the 28th week. It is more often caused by some defect or abnormality of the foetus, or womb, than by the mother's over-activity, or by minor mishaps. To make a note of the time menstruation would normally recur, and to rest as much as possible for two or three days then is wise, for the womb is irritable at that period. Too hot baths, and severe strains, of any kind, emotional or otherwise, should be avoided.

Any flow, however slight, should be regarded seriously and twenty-four hours taken in bed. A threatened miscarriage may be averted by such timely rest, but it is as well always to have a doctor's advice, going to bed and asking him to call. If the miscarriage is inevitable it is even more important to be under expert care.

To sum up, while the mother's health can and should be improved by a pregnancy, rather than the reverse, yet her system is under new strains and weak spots are likely to show up. The earlier any deviations from the normal are tackled the better, so good ante-natal care is very important. But the mother can help herself so much by attending to the simple laws of hygiene and good diet and can confidently expect that, in obeying natural biological laws, her general health will increasingly benefit.

FOR FURTHER READING

Morning Sickness, from 'Mother and Home', 32, Southampton Street, London, W.C.2, 2½d. by post.
Foundations of Motherhood, by C. V. Pink. Cassells, 7s. 6d.

XI

PREPARING FOR THE CONFINEMENT

A DECISION AS to where baby is to be born should be made as soon as pregnancy is established, with the help of the doctor or local Ante-Natal Clinic. Maternity beds and good midwives become booked a long time ahead, and the earlier arrangements can be made the greater the mother's peace of mind.

If baby is to be born in a Maternity Home, or Hospital, the mother will be advised as to what she should bring with her. Everything needed should be collected in good time, and packed in a special case, covering the contents with sterile linen, or well-ironed paper.

If baby is to be born at home, the monthly nurse or midwife should be contacted as soon as possible, so that all arrangements can be discussed well in advance.

The Bed Room

The less furniture in the delivery room the better, but its aspect should be bright and colourings cheery, ready for the convalescing period to follow. In giving a good spring-clean just before the anticipated date, it is sensible to add a little disinfectant to cleansing preparations used. If the room has a carpet, this should be covered with a dust-sheet, fastened down with drugget pins.

A firm bed at a good height makes things easier all round, and sometimes it is possible to hire a bed of a hospital type. Failing this, the home bed can be raised on blocks or strong books. Rails to the bed-head are almost a necessity. The bed should be scrubbed and aired well before use, and the mattress thoroughly protected with mackintosh, or a pad made from several sheets of ironed news-papers, stitched together and inserted in a piece of old sheeting. Four draw-sheets made from old sheeting, about 18 by 54 in. in size, will also be needed.

If the mattress should sag at all, consider using a firm board to prevent this. Place it crosswise under the mattress, just where the buttocks will come, for it is here that a firm base is needed. Space around the bed and good lighting are also points to consider.

For nurse's supplies, it is convenient to instal a small kitchen table, or well-scrubbed trolley, but if a dressing-table is used, it should be protected well. One or two chairs should be in the room, and heating arrangements should be adequate. Other points to bear in mind are that a good supply of hot water will be needed, and that proximity to the lavatory will be labour-saving.

Nurse will advise as to the equipment she will need, and as to what can be borrowed through the local Maternity Clinic. Alternatively, sterile drums, etc., can be purchased from a chemist. Query the provision of apparatus for analgesia. You may not want it, but it is most important that it should be there and that you find it easy to manage. The following items are likely to be needed:

3 doz. sanitary towels (large size).
3 doz. sanitary towels (smaller size).
1 lb. gamgee tissue.
1 lb. cotton wool.
2 sheets of mackintosh:
    1 sheet (1 yard) to go under draw-sheet
    1 sheet (1½ yards) to go on top of mattress.
2 Accouchement sheets.
Large and assorted safety-pins.
Nail-brush.
Bed-pan (Perfection).
2 hot-water bottles.
3 small white enamel bowls.
Feeding-cup.
Medicine glass.
Pure Castile soap.
Bath thermometer.
Olive oil.
Dettol, T.C.P. or Sanitas fluid.
2 large kettles.
A pail or bucket.

Cleanliness
Scrupulous cleanliness is important not only at the time of the confinement itself, and during the lying-in period, but also when

43

getting equipment together. A famous professor has said, 'Dirty hands have destroyed more lives than all the implements of war'. Germs must not be allowed to flourish on any article which the mother or babe may use. Plenty of soap, water and sunshine are the best disinfectants, also a hot iron.

In cleaning the bedroom, a vacuum-cleaner should be used if possible, and a mop with liquid polish; or damp down the carpet, or rug, with wet tea leaves before brushing. Dust first with a damp duster, and polish with a dry one. Remember sunshine is a germicide, so let it come into the room freely.

Adequate domestic arrangements are important if the mother's mind is to be free from worry during the lying-in period. Home Helps can often be obtained to come in daily for a time, so enquire about these at Clinic or Town Hall. To hand over the household reins for at least ten days, preferably for a full month (determining not to be a back-seat-driver from bed), gives the mother the chance to concentrate on baby's running-in period, and to recuperate thoroughly.

XII

BIRTH OF A BABY

THE MORE KNOWLEDGE the mother has of the probable course of events the easier it will be to take them in her stride. First of all, as the expected day of the birth draws near, it is natural for the mother-to-be to wonder how she will be sure when baby has started on his journey, and what she should then do.

Two or three weeks before the day of birth a baby often alters his position, his head sinking forwards and downwards in preparation for entry into the birth canal. This change in his position, known as '*lightening*', makes things more comfortable for the mother, particularly in breathing; but makes walking more arduous, as there is greater pressure on pelvis and thighs.

Warning Signs

There are three possible signs of the actual start of labour. *First* a little plug of mucus, which has sealed the neck of the womb, is loosened and appears streaked with just a little blood. The 'show', as it is called, may precede any noticeable labour pains by twenty-four hours. *Secondly*, a gush of water, or a slow leakage from the birth passage or vagina, will occur if the bag of waters (or membranes) rupture. However, this may not happen until nearly the end of the first stage of labour. Occasionally the waters do not break at all and baby is born completely enclosed in the membranes, or 'caul'—which is considered by the superstitious to be extremely lucky—the real luck of course being that the caul is quickly broken before he is suffocated.

The third sign, the really important one, is a consciousness of the womb's activity, felt at first as small grinding pains in the back passing round to the front. These spasms or contractions will be fleeting, and might be missed, or confused with a spasm due to cramp or colic, were the mother not on the alert. If they are timed, it will be found that there is a definite pattern in their recurrence. As soon as it is established that there is, say, a twenty minute interval between them, she or her husband should report to the midwife or doctor. Contractions will last less than half a minute to begin with, but, to be effective, must increase in frequency and strength and may last up to 80 seconds towards the end of labour.

The First Stage

What is happening is that the top part of the womb is contracting rhythmically in order to push baby on his way; while the neck of the womb is being first pulled up, and then dilated, to make baby's downward passage possible. This so-called 'first stage' of labour may last anything from 12–24 hours with a first baby, so the mother need have no sense of urgency, but she should give those responsible for her care due warning.

The activities of the womb are due to involuntary reflexes and nothing the mother can do will speed them. She can hinder, however, by being tense and frightened, and by getting herself tired and worked-up. Thus she should relax as thoroughly as possible, mentally and physically, and particularly through each 'pain' as it comes. If it is night-time she should go to sleep; if day-time, occupy herself in a pleasant, restful way, taking small, light meals, drinking plenty of water and relieving the bladder frequently.

As the pains get stronger and come more closely together the mother can experiment with various postures, which she will have practised during pregnancy. Kneeling on hands and knees, rounding and hollowing the back and swaying gently forwards and backwards gives comfort, for then the baby's weight presses on the front part of the pelvis instead of on the nerves at the back: or, kneeling, with knees wide apart and with arms resting on pillows on a low chair: or, standing on tiptoe, and leaning forward resting on the bed or its rail.

With longer and more frequent pains (they may last 80 seconds and come every 2 minutes), the mother can cheer herself with the thought that at least half the journey is over. Childbirth has been aptly described as putting a hard but compressible ball through a firm but elastic ring. This needs time and patience. We want the structures to gradually give without tearing, and each pain can accomplish only so much. Massage of the small of the back, either one's self, using one hand at a time, or ideally, by an attendant, is very soothing and sedative.

By means of relaxing many mothers find that though they experience the strong force of each contraction, yet they do not feel any real pain. If, however, they do so, particularly towards the end of the first stage, then it is wise to make use of some form of anaesthesia. Discuss this with nurse in advance and if gas-and-air is to be used, be sure to have trials of it to see that the machine is in good working order. Remember to inhale *before* the expected pain so that its benefit may be felt when the pain is at its height.

The Second Stage

Once the neck of the womb is fully dilated (about 4 in. in diameter) baby enters the vagina and immediately the impulse to bear down, much like straining at stool, is felt. This is the so-called second stage and lasts about an hour and a half with a first baby but much less as a rule with a second one. Now the mother must give up her passive rôle and co-operate fully. She will no longer be able to relax during a pain, but rather will need to make the fullest use of it, seeking however to relax completely in between each to conserve her strength. The feeling of increasing stretching is trying, but knowledge of what is happening steadies her and prevents any feeling of panic, and though she must work very hard, actual pain may still be absent.

Progress is like an incoming tide, each wave receding as well as advancing, because the birth canal is curved and baby has to adjust and adapt in order to get through it.

The mother is usually on the bed at this stage but she need not lie down, but can continue to make use of helpful postures she may have been taught at her ante-natal clinic. She will find for herself which positions give most relief. Remembering that squatting and crouching, time immemorial attitudes for giving birth, make helpful use of the law of gravity, she will not take to her bed too soon. We know ourselves how very difficult it would be, when lying down, to pass a firm stool, and the same muscles are brought into play to bring about the expulsion of the unborn child. Correct breathing is a help. Two or three deep breaths should be taken just before the push commences, and the breath then emitted in a series of short pants.

47

Nurse will instruct her and guide matters so that they are not hurried, especially when the head is first visible, thus seeking to prevent a tear. Once it is free, the shoulders usually follow with the next pain, and then the rest of the baby. Even before the cord is cut the mother can welcome the little stranger by slipping a finger into the little hand, which will at once grasp it tightly. Who can say what sense of safety and of love this may communicate to the child, while on the mother's part the happy contact has a marked effect in causing the womb to contract well. To be fully conscious at this climax is an ideal at which to aim.

The third stage starts after about a quarter of an hour's rest and brings about expulsion of the afterbirth. This usually takes about twenty minutes and leaves the mother with a wonderful feeling of achievement—and of being nice and flat again! The joy of birth is something unique in human experience and more than makes up for what has gone before.

Father's Part

How far can the father share actively in this important crisis in the life of the family?

The idea of being a co-partner in all that pertains to the founding of a family is surely one to be encouraged, and to relegate father to the kitchen, or send him out to distract his mind, does not seem a very good way of arousing his parental instinct and helping him to enter fully into his new responsibilities.

Babies need two parents right the way through from conception to maturity, and though the mother has a physical rôle which cannot be shared, the father's contribution can be a very important one in sustaining and helping her. There should be no barrier put in the way of the father staying with the mother right through labour and being there at the birth to hear the first cry, and see for himself the culmination of the creative partnership which began at conception. The father can be given various useful jobs to do, such as massaging the mother's back, boiling up kettles and generally helping the midwife at her discretion. Naturally, this happy participation will not always be possible, but it is an ideal towards which to aim and will do much to cement family affections.

FOR FURTHER READING

Childbirth Without Fear, by Dr. Grantly Dick Read. Heinemann,
10s. 6d.
The ABC of Natural Childbirth, by Barbara Gelb. Heinemann,
12s. 6d.

XIII

AFTER THE BIRTH

WITH THE BIRTH of her baby the young wife enters a new phase of existence, accompanied by stirring and somewhat bewildering emotions. For a time the whole stream of her being is set towards her child, and the less the outer world intrudes the better she is pleased. Periods of exaltation, however, alternate with those of depression, and this is especially so in the case of the sensitive or highly civilized woman.

If baby cries unduly, if nurse appears unsympathetic or casual, if her husband is late or tactless, she is very ready to dissolve into April tears. Those around her should allow fully for this emotional state—partly due to reaction from strain and fatigue; and partly to glandular changes associated with a complete reversal of previous processes going on in the body.

The fewer visitors the first week the better, and these only the nearest and dearest, who can be trusted not to use her vitality frivolously, nor to burden her with responsibilities, or the need for making decisions.

Convalescence

While she will be guided by those in charge of her care at this time, she will find it easier to co-operate well if she appreciates the tasks which immediately confront her. First the heavy womb, weighing some 2 lb. 2 oz., has to shrink, or involute, until at the end of 6–8 weeks it will weigh only 2–3 oz. The more actively this process goes on at first the better, and breast-feeding sets up reflex uterine contractions which are highly beneficial. Cramp-like after-pains may be troublesome for 24–48 hours, especially with a second pregnancy; but knowing they are doing good, they will be easier to bear, and sedatives to relieve, but not to stop them, can be taken if necessary.

Secondly, the raw surface left by the detachment of the placenta, together with any other lacerations, has to heal. The vaginal discharge (or lochia) is usually abundant and for the first three days consists largely of blood; gradually it changes, becoming first pink, thick and creamy, and then thin and brownish. It usually finishes entirely by the end of 21–24 days.

Nowadays the mother is generally allowed a shower, or even a bath by the fourth day, but care to ensure against risk of infections must be taken until the end of a fortnight.

Thirdly, the tone of the pelvic floor muscles must be restored— the muscles, ligaments and tissues of the pelvis have been loosened and stretched, and there is a risk of prolapse or bladder weakness until these have returned to normal. Not so long ago it was expected that prolapse would occur if the mother should stand too soon, but experience with getting up early seems to point the other way. Today mothers are often advised to sit on the side of the bed and swing foot and leg within a few hours of birth, to improve sluggish circulation; and they may be allowed to stand with support for a brief moment the day following the birth, and are then asked to cough to expand the lungs. They are often allowed to go to the lavatory as early as the third day. By the seventh day they may feel able to bath their own baby and to take a gentle stroll. Hard and fast rules should not be laid down, but the mother who alternates rest with activity convalesces more speedily than one who is too passive.

Exercises in Bed

Bed-exercises should certainly be done, always with the idea of tightening the pelvic floor and the vagina and restoring elasticity to the abdominal muscles. They should be started, with permission, from the second day, beginning just with deep abdominal breathing, and going on to exercise various groups of muscles connected with the feet, the ankles, the thighs, the neck, and especially the pelvic floor and its outlets. Simple contraction—as if holding back either water or a stool—is an effective exercise to practise, and to do this type of movement frequently throughout the day is advised. Again, to lie on the tummy for an hour or so, and to change positions in bed, helps in drainage and involution.

Circling the ankles, and flexing and contracting the foot muscles in bed and while dangling the legs will maintain their tone; and it is also a good plan to make a point of wearing a shoe which gives some support, rather than a sloppy type of bedroom slipper when first getting about.

The so-called lying-in period is usually considered at an end

Exercises following the birth

1. Lying on face, relaxing; alternatively contracting buttocks and thighs tightly together. *Not illustrated*
2. Deep breathing in and out, raising, head and shoulders. *Not illustrated*
3. Deep breathing while on back, to expand the lower part of the chest. Neither the abdomen, nor top part of chest should move.
4. Rounding and stretching spine, clasping knees, and bringing chin to touch them.
5. Raising head, and circling head, neck and shoulders.
6. Bending and then raising each leg alternately; bending and stretching the foot repeatedly while leg is elevated.
7. Raising head and feet, pointing feet well forward, drawing in abdomen.
8. Rising strongly to sitting position, pulling in arches of feet, tightening muscles of the pelvic area.
9. Stretching and limbering the spine in all directions, feet well apart.
10. An exercise to use with the help of an assistant if there is slight backward tilting of the womb.

after a fortnight, but the reproductive organs are not back to normal for at least a further month. The mother must take things as easily as possible during this time and have good, body-building food. She should arrange for a post-natal examination to make sure that all is in order before intercourse is resumed.

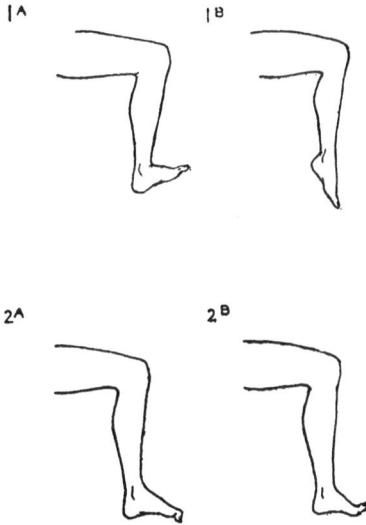

Foot exercises

1. (A and B) Loosening all the joints of toes and ankles by bending, stretching and circling the feet.
2. (A) Pulling up the arch, drawing toes towards the heel. (B) Reverse the movement, drawing heel towards toes.

The period often does not recur for some months if baby is breast-fed, but, if spacing the family is desired, due precautions must be taken.

FOR FURTHER READING

Exercises After Childbirth, 1951, by Gertrude Behn. E. and S. Livingstone, 3s.
Exercises for Use in Convalescence (1), from 'Mother and Home', 32, Southampton Street, London, W.C.2, 2½d. by post.

Exercises for the Figure (2), from 'Mother and Home', 32, Southampton Street, London, W.C.2, 2½d. by post.

Motherhood and the Safe Time Simplified, by L. Lyle Cameron. E. and S. Livingstone, 1s.

The Sex Factor in Marriage, by Dr. Helena Wright, from The National Marriage Guidance Council, 78 Duke Street, London, W.1, 3s. 3d.

Family Spacing

Practical Advice on Family Spacing, The Safe Period. Price 1s.

For Childless Wives. Price 8½d. Family Planning Association, 64, Sloane Street, London, S.W.1.

'Birth Control'—Advice on Family Spacing, by Dr. Helena Wright.

'Letter to a Working Mother.' Price 10½d. by post. Mother's Clinic, 108, Whitfield Street, Tottenham Court Road, London, W.1.

Family Spacing, from 'Mother and Home', 32, Southampton Street, London, W.C.2, 2½d. by post.

XIV

THE NEW ARRIVAL

NONE OF US can remember what it feels like to be introduced into the pageant of life; much loving imagination is needed as we seek ways of softening a baby's first introduction to his new world.

Baby is exchanging a continuously warm, dark, silent, sterile bag of fluid, where everything has been done for him and where he has been protected from every jar, germ, or discomfort, for a comparatively chilly, noisy, glaring and airy place. Hands touch and lift him; material is wrapped round the sensitive skin, light gets to the eyes, moving and cool air to the face and into the lungs, and, of a sudden, he is asked to begin a wholly independent existence. No wonder he cries, thus expelling fluids, filling the lungs with oxygen and starting his breathing mechanism on a task which we will hope it will perform satisfactorily for at least three-score-years-and-ten. Other mechanisms, lying dormant, must soon be called into service—the heat—regulating centres, the digestive system, and so on. How these are 'run in' that first week of life is going to tell vitally in the future. Baby is free from all prejudice in the matter, though he has some fugitive impulses and inherited behaviour patterns. Good impulses can be strengthened and turned into habit by repetition—less desirable ones allowed to fade out through disuse.

Warmth, sterility and quiet are vital needs. For the first hours of life the aim must be to reproduce as far as possible the conditions under which baby has been living in the womb. Even then, there is of necessity so much that must be entirely new to him. The receiving blanket should be wrapped round a hot-water bottle until it is required, and it is best if a soft square of butter muslin, or a Harrington napkin, is tacked inside it for softness. The temperature of the room should be about 65° and the cot stood in a draught-proof corner, with a screen around it to cut off bright light. A covered hot-water-bottle, placed between the blankets, or under the mattress, will warm the cot ready to receive him.

Breathing

Doctor or nurse will clear nose or mouth, should it be necessary, to see that there is a proper airway to enable baby to breathe, but it will be some time before the lungs function really efficiently. Breathing is rapid, shallow, and often irregular in the first weeks. Its efficient establishment is helped by due mothering, fondling, carrying about, and by occasionally tipping the head downwards to bring a flow of oxygenated blood to the brain. The risk of suffocation in the early days, before baby has the strength to alter his position, or throw back a cover if it works up over his face, is very real, and the mother needs to be closely observant.

First Stools

Nature ensures that the bowel learns its function in a simple, easy way. A mucus, known as meconium, of a greeny-black colour, accumulates in the intestines before birth in sufficient quantities to afford seven or eight good stools. In this way material is provided on which to practise the necessary mechanical act of evacuation without any sort of strain being imposed on the system.

First Food

The introduction to the vital processes of suckling and digesting is also made as easy as possible. The colostrum, or pre-milk, present at birth is practically identical in composition with the food on which baby has been nourished in his ante-natal life. Quickly it establishes the suckling activity without burdening the digestive tract. This is thus taught to tolerate a fluid content, which changes from day to day, until it is normal breast milk. These lessons in digestion are a very important part of baby's introduction to life.

THE NEW BORN

Next to the thrill of receiving her precious baby into her arms, comes the happy occasion when the mother is able to inspect all his charms, free from muffling shawls and other coverings.

The first thing she will notice is what a grown-up and individual little face he has—the idea that all new-borns look much alike has no foundation in fact!

The New Arrival

Generally he looks 'old for his age', and that is because the little face is not well covered with fat, and the underlying structures show more than they will do when baby is two or three months older. He often looks amazingly like some adult relation at this stage, but this likeness may completely change as he grows.

Some babies are born with a thick crop of hair which will in all probability be the final hue of the hair in later life. This first hair usually rubs off in a few weeks, and is gradually replaced by fairer hair, which lasts throughout childhood but darkens as the child gets older. On the other hand, quite a proportion are born bald, and it may take some months to grow enough hair to justify the use of a brush.

The wise mother early acquaints herself with baby's make-up, training herself to observe him in detail, so that she can notice at once if anything is out of the ordinary. It is often surprising how some condition, which should have called for early treatment, has been overlooked, simply because the mother was unobservant, or ignorant of its significance.

Such things as the beginning of scurf, some tiny swelling, spots and pimples, difficulties in breathing, a bad colour, blue lips, and a protrusion anywhere need noting, without of course a sense of worry. Birth marks usually force themselves on the attention. These are frequently due to pressure during the actual birth, and will fade away quite soon. Other types of skin markings, however, may be more persistent, and if they increase in size in relation to skin area, specific measures to remove them may prove necessary later on (see p. 204).

Then it is possible that the baby's breasts will be swollen. This glandular activity frequently occurs in both boy and girl babies. As a general rule it will die away of itself; but, until it does so, mothers and nurses should be particularly careful to lift baby by slipping the hands underneath its body, and not under the arm-pits, where some pressure over the breast region is unavoidable. As there is a possibility of infection occurring through the nipple when such activity is present, until it subsides it will be wise to cover each breast with a small square of lint, lightly held in place with a gauze bandage.

If labour has been somewhat prolonged, the tissues at the top of baby's head may appear slightly swollen, and the head may appear a little misshapen, while, if forceps have been necessary, there may be a swollen bump. All these troubles will right themselves without any interference as a rule, and there is nothing to worry about in them. It is a good plan to try and give the little head fairly equal pressure by regularly changing the side baby sleeps on.

The First Toilet

The modern plan of postponing the first bath until the cord is healed at 9 or 10 days old has much to commend it. This leaves the salve-like cream, with which the baby is covered at birth (the vernix caseosa) undisturbed—a protection against possible infections—while baby's energies are not dissipated nor chilling risked. The protective covering disappears of itself in about 48 hours, and meanwhile baby's little face can be made presentable and the buttocks given a toilet when necessary, using sterile gauze or cotton wool, dipped in sterile water, from a bowl previously boiled to reduce risk of infections to the lowest minimum.

The Soft Spot

The so-called 'soft spot' at the top of baby's head is where pieces of bone that go to make up the top of the skull have not yet grown together, thus enabling the head to mould itself to the birth passage. The area involved varies, and is liable to increase at first with the growth of the head, and then it will begin to close up, being completely closed between the twelfth and twenty-fourth month, according to its original size, and to baby's general health.

BABY'S INSTINCTS

The new-born baby has two special fears—that of falling and of loud noises, possibly associated with birth experiences. He has strong instincts connected with self-preservation and love.

When baby is happy at the breast, these two instincts are being satisfied harmoniously at one and the same time, but, alas, too often anxiety comes in at feeding-times. Sometimes it is just that the mother is not very observant and does not hold him so that he gets the nipple easily, without having his nasal passages blocked; sometimes the milk gushes out so freely that he chokes and splutters; sometimes he is asked to work hard on an empty breast, and becomes discouraged. Hints to help mothers over these and similar difficulties are given on pp. 70–75.

Holding Baby

Again, because of his fears, mother must look to the way she handles baby. She should never snatch baby up either with a zealous intention of saving a napkin, or with an outburst of uncontrolled 'mother love'. Nor should she pick him up so casually that he has no sense of firm security. Instead she should use her imagination to appreciate what it must feel like to be lifted by giant hands out of a warm couch, and to be carried about without a sense of real support.

The best way of lifting a baby is to slip one hand under the head and along the back, and to speak to him quietly before raising him gently. Compared to a sudden pick up, this may be likened to the effect of a steady English lift, rather than a breath-taking New York elevator!

When carrying a baby up and down stairs, one hand should be over him, and one under as support. In laying him down, the mother should bend down well and keep her arms under him for a few seconds until he has relaxed in his nest. Proper handling of baby soothes and stabilizes the nervous system, reducing anxiety, and making it easy for him, when awake, to lie and amuse himself happily.

The Nervous System

While much progress has been made in the physical care of babies in the last decade, yet nervous strains tend to be on the increase. Recognizing this, the parents should try and surround the newcomer with a quiet and stable environment, so that the nervous system has little to tax it before it is more mature.

While there is no need to worry about average domestic sounds, voices should be modulated, and banging doors, blaring wireless and sudden bursts of loud noises eschewed. If the mother is strung up and nervy, she should try to make time to lie on her bed and relax well before she picks baby up for a feed.

Baby has experienced absolute peace and quiet in the pre-natal existence, and his sense of hearing is both acute and sensitive in the early months. He should be accustomed gradually to varying sounds and have long periods of real peacefulness each day.

59

Early Impressions

A baby takes joy and comfort from the sound of his mother's voice, and if she talks to him as nursery routines are carried out it will develop his intelligence and give reassurance. He will soon show his delight in his mother's presence, stretch out his arms towards her and generally repay her richly for all the care and love lavished on him. Never try and force or overstimulate him, however. Babies have moods as well as adults, and may be robbed of vitality and stability if responses are sought too frequently.

The mother's gaiety and friendliness and firmness and gentleness are going to mean a tremendous amount to her child. Please do not think he is too young to 'notice' or to 'understand', but treat him as a personality—and not a cross between a pet or a robot—from the very first day of his existence!

The sleepy little baby in his cradle is not going to drop his babyhood as a snake drops its skin; he will merely grow gradually from one stage into the next. Impressions made on his subconscious mind, even in the earliest, least responsive days, are not easily obliterated. The first months, when baby is so malleable and unprejudiced, are golden days for forming foundation habits, which —in essence, if not in expression—will last for life.

NAMING YOUR CHILD

A name is a handle the individual presents to his world. There should be nothing about it which needs explanation, nor which causes a look of surprise, incredulity, or disapproval to creep into the face of anyone who hears it for the first time. In choosing baby's name visualize him as a small boy (or girl), facing his contemporaries; as a grown man using his initials. Say the proposed names aloud, linked with the surname; write down the initials they form. Ask yourself how the name is likely to be shortened; what nickname it suggests; is it easy to spell and to pronounce?

Avoid—particularly for a girl—names linked to a particular year, or those which, through their historical or literary associations, have an unpleasant flavour. It hardly seems sense to choose names which are just adjectives describing the surname—such as Rose Tree. Or names which are very obvious such as Peter Piper or Jack Horner! Anything in the nature of a pun or joke should be steadfastly refused!

Of the two names chosen—and two seems the ideal number—put first the one you mean to use for the child. Try and find out the meanings of the names. Present his name to your baby as a token of the high hopes you have for him. Knights of old chose their titles with care, and parents should consider how far the names they are choosing will help or hinder a child as he goes through life.

FOR FURTHER READING

Naming Your Baby, by Elsdon Smith. Allenson Co., Ltd., 3s. 6d.
Signposts for Baby, from 'Mother and Home', 32, Southampton Street, London, W.C.2, 2½d. by post.

XV

BABY'S BATH AND TOILET

THE DAILY BATH should be a treat both for the bather and his
mother. Children are never so sweet as when kicking and splashing
away, thoroughly enjoying their miniature sea. If, however, the
mother is nervous or rushed, she will communicate her fears and
tensions to baby and the joy will go, leaving only a troublesome
piece of routine.

The first point to remember is that young babies lose heat very
rapidly. Everything should be in readiness before a single garment
is removed, so that, once the rite is started, it may be 'full steam
ahead' until baby is clothed again. All windows should be closed,
the room warmed if necessary (not above 70° F.) and any draughts
dealt with efficiently. A three-fold screen is helpful in making a cosy
corner if the room is a large one. The bath should be on a stand, or
on chairs, both to be away from floor draughts and to save unnecessary stooping. As baby gets older and more energetic, it is a good
plan to stand the tub on a stool inside the big bath, so that splashes
do not matter. Promote to the big bath, if possible, by the time he is
six months old, so that he can 'swim' freely with your support.
There is a new bath on the market, the Poppet, which fits inside
the big bath so that it can be filled from the taps and emptied very
easily (see p. 34).

Before the bath is filled, a trolley, with basket holding all baby's
utensils, including a small enamel bowl of boiled water, and a pail
of water in readiness for soiled napkins, should be put near at hand.
Preparations for the feed to follow, whether bottle or breast-fed,
should also be made, and the pram got ready.

Temperature
Tepid water should go into the bath first (unless the correct temperature can be mixed in the jug), then, when hot or cold has been
added, the whole should be stirred around before the bath thermo-

meter is read, or the water tested with the elbow. Blood-heat is right for the small baby's bath—as near the temperature of the waters in which he floated before birth as you can make it. The right temperature is important, for, quite apart from the risks of chilling or scalding baby, if the bath strikes him on his sensitive skin in an un-pleasant way, he is liable to take a dislike to it which may take a long time to overcome.

If the water is hard it should be softened—boiled rain-water is the ideal. A little borax, a bag of oatmeal, Calgon, or other suitable softener can be used in small quantities; remember how delicate and fine a baby's skin is.

Face cloths can be made from squares of soft muslin. These should be provided with a tape, hung up be-tween use and boiled once a week. Body cloths can be made of towelling. Swabs of cotton wool can also be used and burnt. If the mother cannot resist the charms of a sponge, it should be frequently soaked in boiled water to which a drop or two of ammonia has been added. It is best not to use one on the face, and certainly baby must not be allowed to suck his sponge!

Before picking baby up the mother should protect her clothing with a mackintosh or plastic apron, covered with one of towelling or flannel; remove all rings and brooches, and wash her hands thoroughly.

BABY'S BATH

'Scrub everything in the house except the baby' is a useful slogan. A small baby is delightfully clean, and if the buttocks are washed separately, very little soap will be needed. Only a pure super-fatted soap should be used and to gently pass a soapy hand over each little limb in turn—in the direction of the heart—is all that is usually necessary. The soap must be carefully rinsed off afterwards.

Nature has her own way of keeping a baby's eyes, nose, ears and mouth clean, although they may need help from time to time. Separate swabs of sterile cotton wool and boiled water can be used for the eyes, wiping gently from the nose edge outwards. If there is any discharge, the doctor should be asked about it at once.

In the ears there are tiny invisible hairs which very slowly move the protecting wax outwards. Wax which appears in the outer ear can be gently removed, but all poking must be avoided.

Hairs, again, sweep dust-laden mucus in the nasal passages downwards; often when the larger hairs nearer the openings are reached, baby experiences a tickle and gives a hearty sneeze. It is important to keep the nasal passages clear so that baby can be trained to be a nose and not a mouth breather. Gently to stroke the outer sides of the nose downwards to encourage a sneeze, before baby is old enough to blow his nose, is a sensible procedure. A twist of cotton wool or one of Johnson's cotton tips can be used occasionally.

Now for the order of the bath. The face should be washed first with baby's own special soft wash-cloth and dried gently. The scalp is then washed with a soapy hand, rinsed well over the bath and dried. During the shampoo, baby's head should be supported with the palm of the mother's left hand, his shoulders resting on the forearm. The scalp is usually washed every day at first, then every other day; while at about 6 months, once a week is sufficient.

Wash baby with a soapy hand as necessary while on the lap and he is now ready to go into the water. To hold firmly and yet comfortably, the left hand should pass under his head so that the left shoulder and arm are supported. The right hand can either pick up the ankles, or go under the buttocks. Lifting and lowering should be managed gently, with no jerky movements, and it is good to talk and smile while doing so.

Once in the bath, a little water can be gently splashed over the chest and any other parts which may be exposed. Then baby is turned over, supporting his chest with the left hand and forearm.

To squeeze water on to his spine from some little height is strengthening to the back muscles. The length of time he is allowed to stay in the water depends on his age, the warmth of the room, and his general health; mothers must use their common sense in this matter.

To lift baby out of the bath, his two ankles are picked up with the right hand, and, with the left under his shoulders he is laid on the towel on the lap, and then turned towards the mother, face downwards. The ends of the towel are brought over him, and he is gently blotted, rather than rubbed or dried. Now feel him everywhere to ensure there is no damp area. If a little powder is to be used, to shake it on the hand and then apply lightly prevents any clogging of the pores. If there is any chafing, or tenderness, a lotion, or medicated mineral oil may be needed for a while, a little being poured on the hand and then applied.

DRESSING BABY

Baby's little garments will be warming during the bath in the order in which they will be needed. Dress him swiftly and deftly to avoid chilling and discomforts.

Because his head is more egg-shaped than round, be sure to pass head-openings—which should be nice and wide—over the back of the head and then slip down swiftly over the face. Baby will not like having his view obliterated a moment longer than is necessary!

While still on his back, the napkin should be applied in one of the ways described on p. 66. Pin to a tab on the vest to prevent tearing. Bootees can also be put on at this stage if wished. They may not be needed.

Now slip first petty and then frock over the head and turn in order to do both up together. The matinee jacket, if one is needed, can then be laid in position over his back, and he can be turned back to complete his toilet. Stretch the sleeves with thumb and two fingers to make wide openings to pass over the little arms.

Fastenings at neck, wrist and ankles should be firm enough to prevent the entry of cold air, but not tight enough to constrict in any way. If you find your baby's skin marked, however faintly, when he is undressed, you should make adjustments to the fastenings to prevent this.

Do not sit baby up while dressing him until he is strong enough

65

to hold his head erect unaided, and be careful not to compress the little chest and nipples.

PUTTING ON THE NAPPIES

There are various ways of applying the napkin and mothers will like to experiment to find the most efficient. The most usual method is to fold the soft muslin napkin into a triangle, folding once, twice, or even three times, according to the size of both baby and the napkin. Put the straight end under baby, and join all the

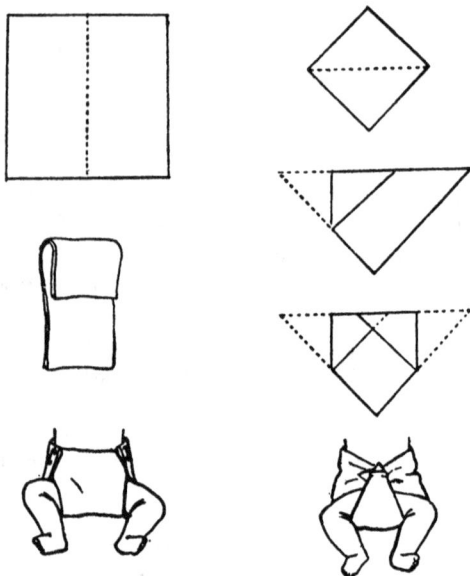

FIG 1   FIG 2

three corners in front, fastening with one strong safety-pin, Fig. 2. For extra protection, a turkish towelling napkin can be wrapped around outside.

Alternatively, fold the napkin oblong fashion, either in half or in three. Turn down one end about 5 in. Use this doubled end under a baby girl, and in front with a baby boy. Bring the two thinner ends between the legs, and fasten on either side with a safety-pin to make a neat pilch, Fig. 1. Whatever method chosen, remember the aim is to give the maximum of protection with the minimum of bulk between the legs.

The Cold Sponge

After six months it is a good plan to introduce a cool and then a cold sponge down after the warm bath. This closes the pores of the skin and is tonic to the whole system. Cold water constricts all the surface blood vessels and drives the blood inwards to the lungs, etc. After it, if there is a good reaction, the constricted vessels dilate, and there comes a rush of arterial blood to the surface, leaving the skin glowing and the whole metabolism invigorated.

The warm bath, on the other hand, is of special value to the nervous, over-tired, over-excited, or chilled child. Warm water opens superficial blood vessels, sets the heart beating more quickly, and brings blood away from the internal organs. It increases the frequency of the pulse and releases tension, and thus is a good prelude to sleep. Care must be taken after one to prevent chilling as all the vessels and pores will be dilated and relaxed and the skin giving off perspiration.

BATHING THE TODDLER

Modifications to this bath-time routine will develop as baby grows, and the bath can be happily used for teaching independence and fresh skills. The toddler will delight in his own miniature soap and washing-cloth, and, given a chance, will scrub himself heartily, if ineffectively. Don't impede this activity because his standard of cleanliness is rather sketchy. The wise mother bottles up her efficiency, and lets baby develop his in the only possible way—by learning how through practice.

Here is the toddler's ideal tub. The business part is done first. He should stand up to the job—preferably using a foot tub or something of the kind if he is very grubby—so that the bath itself is kept soap-free and clean. Provide two or three terry towelling cloths. One can be for the child's use; one kept strictly for the face; another for the body. These cloths should be frequently boiled. (There are two objections to sponges—delightful as they are for squeezing water and for their feel and texture—you can't boil them; and they do not give the skin much friction.) Tackle face and ears first, neck and hands; then the body, giving light but efficient attention to all the parts; the child should then sit down so that his feet can be washed thoroughly, the older child using a loofah or nail-brush for the purpose. Now the bath can be enjoyed; if the hair is longish, a cap should be worn and aquatic feats encouraged. The child who doesn't mind ducking and submerging in the safety of the bath-room is getting ready thoroughly to enjoy later seaside experiences. If he revels in a cold douche before he emerges it will be splendid for his circulation.

Encourage the child to dry himself, providing a special towel for the purpose so that he keeps himself warm and increases his personal responsibility at the same time.

Remember that bath-time is examination time. Under cover of washing and drying the mother can see that woollies are not irritating delicate skins, elastics are not too tight, or that heat spots or rashes are not appearing on the little body.

XVI

BREAST-FEEDING

BREAST-FEEDING SHOULD be a boon to mother and child. It is the ideal method of nutrition for the individual baby, and a bulwark against many infections while he is too weak to combat these. It aids the return of the womb to normal, and prevents degenerative changes in the breast. Through it the mother's maternal instincts receive their full satisfaction, and the tender link between herself and her baby is warmly strengthened. As the small baby sleeps so much of his day, waking principally for his feeds, these mean a tremendous amount to him; no early impressions could be more blissful than being in his mother's arms and sucking at her breast. Such impressions are retained in the unconscious part of the memory and play their part in the building of personality.

Watch a well-fed baby asleep and you will note the little mouth working away in an ecstatic sucking dream. The wrongly-fed baby may mouth and seek in agitated fashion. In the one case there is a bent towards tension and anxiety; in the other towards confidence and peace.

A good flow of milk depends on three things. First, a good nipple; second, baby's well co-ordinated efforts to obtain his nourishment; and third, the mother's emotional and physical state and attitude of mind towards her child. It is far more important to make breast-feeding enjoyable to both mother and baby, and to carry it out in an atmosphere free from tension and worry, than it is to watch the clock, or the scales.

Breast milk is more readily digested than other milks because it and the infant's stomach have been made for each other. It is always at blood heat and contains no harmful bacteria. It supplies the tender tissues with vitamins and hormones and nutrients in due proportion. It has never been completely copied in the laboratories

69

because it is a living, highly complex food of just the right elements needed for an individual baby's healthy development.

A wise diet (see p. 7) and a sensible arrangement of the day helps to keep the milk at its best. Baby's regular suction helps to maintain the quantity he needs.

Care of Nipples

Should the nipples crack—though with care this should not occur —it is best to express milk by hand, or use an all-rubber nursing nipple, rather than let baby go directly to the breast when pain and damage would follow. Cod-liver oil, or a soothing and healing ointment can be applied to them in between feeds, and removed very gently before the following feed. Do not make the mistake of leaving the breast full of milk, for this might be likely to lead to a breast abscess—a far more serious condition.

As a routine, the nipple and areola should be swabbed with boiled water before being given to baby, so that it is as clean as possible, and after the feed it should be again gently wiped over and dried thoroughly. Scrupulous cleanliness of this nature, together with cold sponging, will make nipple troubles unlikely to occur. It is a wise plan to pin a clean square of boiled linen or fold of lint to the undergarment next the skin, renewing this each day.

In establishing breast-feeding there will be two specially tricky times. (1) The first running-in, when the mother is inexperienced and often a prey to fears. (2) When she first gets about and takes up the threads of normal living again, and is easily over-tired.

In the earliest stage one of the most important factors is comfort. The mother should enjoy having her baby in her arms, hold him cosily and let him touch her soft breast. Baby must be given time to feel quite at home. All sense of urgency must be banished. Every baby suckles in a slightly different way from every other and Nurse's task is to remove obstacles, but she should interfere as little as possible and not to urge baby on if he is not yet ready to suckle.

If he opens his mouth and takes the nipple when put to the breast both mother and nurse can rejoice; but if he does not do so, no one should worry. Expressing a drop or two of fluid into his mouth may start the good work, but nothing remotely connected with force should be used to cajole him.

70

Running-In

Baby comes well nourished into the world and needs nothing, apart from a little water, for the first week. Put him to the breast by all means—so that the suckling reflex has a good chance to become established, and so that he may get the colostrum, designed to educate the digestive tract before the milk comes in—but don't be worried if things don't go as smoothly as you'd hoped.

Try not to over-feed in the early days if the milk comes in strongly. All baby's organs are immature, and, though possetting may relieve the situation temporarily, when this occurs frequently it means that they are under unnecessary strain.

Fluctuations

The next stage is more difficult. When the mother starts being active or returns home, round about the tenth to fourteenth day, she is quite likely to 'lose her milk' temporarily. Ideally she should go more slowly, have no responsibilities, other than the care of baby for at least a month. (Remember it takes six weeks for the womb to return to normal.) But, if this is not possible—and for many mothers it isn't—then she must not panic, but realize that the 'frightened' milk will come in again with a little coaxing.

At this period she needs all the encouragement she can get. More rest, good feeding, more sense of being backed and helped by those around, more assurance that things will come right. She herself can help by emptying the breasts by hand after feeds if it does not tire her. She should never attempt to 'save up' the milk—stripping steps it up; hoarding diminishes it.

Improving the Flow

Efforts to stimulate the supply (see p. 73) should continue hopefully, remembering that not only is the milk sometimes delayed for many days, but that cases have been known when a baby has not been put to the breasts for several weeks, and yet the supply has been brought in fully. Always remember that half a loaf is better than no bread and do not be tempted to wean because of insufficiency.

Two more points! Free baby's little arms so that the little hands can gently knead and massage the breast as baby suckles. Nothing stimulates the flow as well as this. And be sure baby can breathe easily—not only by seeing that there is a clear airway to the nose, but, if yours is an active breast, by seeing that he does not get choked. Tone your nipples with cold splashing; or apply just enough pressure on their base to close the ducts partially if the flow is very free. With some mothers the draught reflex, as it is called, is felt strongly, and the milk may spurt out before baby starts suckling. In such cases it will be wise to draw off just a little milk by hand.

Sleepy Feeders

Some babies seem strangely indifferent to the charms of food and prefer to be left in peace at feed times. The persistent way in which these small folk fall asleep at the breast is, to say the least of it, discouraging. It is a good rule with every baby to see that he is 'wakened all over', if one may use the expression, before he starts his feed. To sting him awake by tapping or shaking would be foolish and harmful. The wakening should be gentle but thorough —cool moving air, brighter light, change of posture, with firm quiet handling, will do what is required.

Perhaps baby starts well but soon tires of sucking. Yet, when taken away, the milk will come quite easily with a little pressure. Why is this? It may be that baby is using up too much vitality in maintaining his hold on the nipple. See that you hold him in such a way that the head and whole of the spine is well supported and so that the nipple is lowered into the mouth rather than baby needing to reach up to it. It may be that he is troubled with wind, which is often swallowed while feeding if baby is too eager or too lazy.

Sometimes the best way of dealing with the poor sucker is to just slightly shorten the time allowed at the breast, ending the meal with expressed breast-milk from spoon, pipette, or bottle. This gives him his full nutriment without encouraging bad sucking habits, or marring the rhythm of his rests.

72

Wind

All babies swallow a certain amount of 'wind' and it is important to give them opportunities of releasing any air bubble in the intestines at intervals. To feed the baby in a semi-upright position so that the wind comes up easily may help. Make a habit, too, of holding baby against your left shoulder for a minute or two when he is first picked up before the feed starts. After he has finished with one breast hold him up again comfortably before changing sides. Then again at the end of the feed, before you settle him down. The actual time needed will vary. Try a slight shift of posture and a little gentle back rubbing if the 'burp' is delayed.

If baby is really and truly imbibing milk as he suckles you will both see and hear the process, but baby may sometimes use the nipple as a dummy, enjoying himself at the time but, alas, waking hungry and windy an hour or so later. Test-weighing in such cases may prove that the so-called 'good feed', of twenty minutes or so, had given baby a net nutriment of one ounce or less.

Whether breast or bottle-fed, baby will make a better meal if outward disturbances are reduced to the minimum. You may not always be able to feed him alone, but arrange to cut off a cosy corner for him, and try to give him your affectionate attention. Babies are very sensitive and soon feel cheated if mother's thoughts and eyes are elsewhere. If the mother is tense and nervous, to feed baby on a cushion helps, cutting off some of the electric contact between the two.

Insufficient Milk

If baby gains less than four ounces a week, several weeks in succession, it is probable that he is not getting enough milk. Before introducing a complement—which will tend to alter the flora of the intestines—the flow should be stimulated in three main ways.

First—extra rest. Earlier bed, a longer mid-day rest, more peaceful meals, a better position during feeds, will all help; as well as mental relaxation, dropping all worries as far as possible.

Secondly, an improved diet. The nutrients that baby is taking from the milk must be replaced. Vitamin B in the form of two tablespoonfuls of Bemax, a raw egg beaten in milk may help. A glass of water with each feed ensures a good fluid intake.

Thirdly, local stimulation to the breasts. Have two bowls, one containing hot water, and one cold, and a separate cloth in each. Bathe each breast first in cold, and then in the hot, alternating quickly, for about 5 minutes. Then dry briskly from without towards the nipple. Massage is also useful in promoting a flow of blood to the parts, and thereby stimulating good secretion. It also helps to bring the milk forward, thus making it possible for new supplies of milk to form in the emptying glands. Use the whole palm of the hand and from above, below, and the sides, stroke with light but steady pressure, always towards the nipple from the outer border, supporting the breast with the unused hand.

Expect the flow to improve, but do not be downhearted if it seems rather static. Breast milk is a good pre-digester of other foods, and to partially feed is much better than to wean.

Test-weighing

Test-weighing occasionally may be helpful, both in assessing whether the supply is improving, and also in deciding the amount of complement baby needs for good nutrition.

For this reliable scales are needed (not spring balances), and half-ounce weights. Pop baby on the scales before a feed, and, as soon as he has finished, put him on them once more, without so much as removing a safety-pin. The difference between the two weights will be the amount in fluid ounces baby has imbibed.

It is natural for quite differing amounts to be taken at differing times of day, so test-weighing must be followed round the clock before any definite conclusions can be reached. As a very rough guide, the average baby, after the first ten days, needs about $2\frac{1}{2}$–$2\frac{3}{4}$ fluid ounces to each pound of body-weight a day.

If not convenient to test-weigh at all feeds, reckon that baby will take about twice the amount at 6 a.m. as at 2 p.m. At 10 p.m. he is likely to take about a quarter more than he does at 2 p.m.

Gain and Stools
To provide sufficient milk for nourishment is not all that is needed.

Food which gives rise to colicky indigestion, or which over-stimulates so that sleep is restless, or which over-develops so that tissues become flabby and heavy, takes serenity from babyhood and from motherhood too.

Here is where a study of the stools and a careful record of gains in weight are important. There is usually an initial loss of a few ounces during the first week in life and this is gradually made good, so that the birth-weight will be regained by the tenth to fourteenth day. The week's gain will then probably be round about 6–8 ounces for the next three months. After that it will slow down a little. Study the weight table on p. 228.

The stools after the first few days should be a bright orange colour, smooth, soft and somewhat like made mustard. Anything up to four a day may be considered normal in the first months. Loose, green, frothy, curdy, scanty or very frequent stools are a sign that adjustments are needed. Delayed stools usually have little significance and just mean baby is absorbing his food well and that there is little residue to provide bulk. Curdy stools point to a difficulty in digesting fat.

Quality of Milk

Is the quality of breast milk ever at fault? It may be if diet and hygiene are poor. Little however can be told by looking at the milk and no analysis will give reliable information unless a really good, mixed sample is obtained. To provide this it will be necessary to express milk at the beginning, the end, and at various in-between stages of feeds, over a period of 24 hours.

Recent tests have pointed in some cases to a fat deficiency, which may account for a failure to satisfy an older baby. To see that he strips the breasts is important, as the richer milk comes at the end of the feed. In other cases, however, it is an excess of fat which has led to restlessness and vomiting. Less fat in the mother's diet and more exercise is then indicated, and baby should have a little water with feeds.

Vitamins

The mother should be on the alert to take vitamins regularly in her diet (see p. 9). As an added precaution it is advised that, from the age of six weeks, or earlier if the mother's health is poor, fruit

75

juice, to ensure a supply of vitamin C should be given daily. The Government supply a concentrated form of orange juice which can be procured at Welfare Clinics and other distributing centres at a low price. Fresh orange juice, swede juice, rose hips, or tomato juice are alternatives. Start with a drop or two, in a teaspoon of water, and increase until baby is having four teaspoons of juice to four of water at three to four months of age.

Vitamins A and D can be started at about the same time. The Government Cod-Liver Oil Compound is the cheapest way of providing these. Begin with two drops, and work up gradually to a level teaspoon in about a month's time, given before the 10 a.m. feed.

Or give a reliable emulsion, in which the fat globules are more finely subdivided. In this case start with a quarter of a teaspoon, and work up to three teaspoons a day if baby tolerates it well.

If you are anxious not to increase the amount of fat baby is taking, the vitamins can be given in a synthetic preparation, such as Adexolin, starting with one drop given three times a day, increasing to three drops given thrice daily.

Vitamin B in the form of a yeast extract can be begun at about three months. See the chapter on Early Extras, p. 85.

FOR FURTHER READING

Baby's Birthright, by Doris Anderson. Faber & Faber, 5s.
Weight Chart, from 'Mother and Home', 32, Southampton Street, London, W.C.2, 2½d. by post.

XVII

BOTTLE-FEEDING

IF BABY HAS to be reared 'by hand', as we say, naturally the choice of a good substitute for breast milk is a matter of great importance. Some mothers are content blindly to follow a formula, but the majority like to know more about the whys and wherefores, in order to make intelligent adjustments and avoid possible mistakes.

The milk of every mammal varies in the proportions of the constituents —water, protein, carbohydrate, fat, minerals and vitamins it contains. The baby whale in the ocean wilds, the new calf in the farmstead, the baby rabbits in the warren, a baby elephant in the jungle, are all started in life by means of a living, easily digested fluid food, to ensure growth, warmth and energy, which, while similar in content, has proportions adapted to the environment and life history of each.

The baby whale needs special warmth, so his mother's milk contains twelve times the amount of fat found in breast milk. The baby rabbit should double his birth-weight in a week so his mother manufactures milk which contains ten to fifteen times more protein. The elephant has a large frame to fill and his mother's milk is far richer in all ways than is human milk.

Cow's Milk

Artificially-fed babies in this country are nearly always given cow's milk in one form or another. Experience has shown that, with due modification, this milk will suit the vast majority—there are a few who are allergic to it and need special alternatives.

The calf takes six to seven weeks to double its birth-weight and it

77

possesses a very special type of stomach. It is natural then that cow's milk should contain some three times the amount of protein —the growth and body-building factor—than human milk, also that much of this protein should be of a tough consistency. On the other hand, the human baby, with his wider field of activity, is in greater need of energizers than the calf, so breast milk contains over 2 per cent more sugar. The fat in each case is roughly the same. With breast milk as our guide, an attempt must be made to adapt milk designed by nature for a calf to suit a human infant.

Protein

By boiling the cow's milk the curd is softened considerably. By adequately diluting it, the protein content matches human growth. In so diluting, however, we reduce the level of the sugar and the fat, as well as some of the minerals. Hence we have to make suitable additions.

Sugar

There are various forms of sugar on the market. Sugar of milk has definite advantages to offer, and is the sugar of choice for the first months of life. As the milk is gradually strengthened, so the amount of added sugar is reduced, until, when whole milk is given, no added sweetening is required.

Fat

It is important that the extra fat is well divided and not taken all at once. It is a good plan to measure the day's supply into a small jar and to give a one-fifth portion with each feed. As well as restoring the balance of fat in the mixture, we have to bear in mind that baby needs protective elements, and thus must choose a fat rich in vitamins A and D. Fish eat small green plants growing in sun-kissed, oxygen-laden water. The vitamins obtained from these are stored in their fat, liver and roe. In our often sunless climate some form of fish oil, or its equivalent, should be offered to baby daily. Most babies tolerate and even enjoy, pure cod-liver oil, but, when emulsified, the fat globules of such oils are finely sub-divided and the whole rendered specially palatable. It is important to be sure that such an emulsion contains 40 or 50 per cent oil and is well standardized. After the first weeks, butter can be used as part of the fat, if wished, adding vitamins in the form of cod-liver oil, or halibut oil, or a synthetic vitamin preparation. There is no virtue in giving more than the prescribed dose of cod-liver oil and an excess can do harm.

Vitamin C, to ensure the fresh element, is also needed and can be given as orange juice, rose-hip syrup, blackcurrant syrup, tomato or swede juice. See p. 76.

Types of Milk

The milk itself can be fresh, obtained from a mixed T.T. herd (Jersey milk is too rich for the young baby, as a rule); or it can be dried by the spray process, which has the advantage of avoiding excessive heat; or by being poured on to hot rollers, when the fluid is driven off and solid constituents remain; or condensed by evaporating much of the water and sterilizing. It is important to know what additions, if any, have already been made to a branded milk, and to have a reliable formula to follow. If fresh milk is used, it must always be brought to the boil in the home. Remember, no matter how good and clean the milk, or milk powder, it is possible for it to become infected in the home. Thus, all milk for baby must be kept in a cool place and well covered to protect it from dust.

If using a dried milk, care in measuring is important, lifting the powder lightly, not packing down, and levelling to the spoon's edge with a knife. If household spoons are used, check with a chemist, to ensure that the size is correct, and keep labelled for baby's use.

Bottles

For the necessary equipment, if possible get bottles with a wide top. Not only are they easy to clean, but the type of nipple which goes with them more closely resembles the breast, and gives baby good jaw exercise. In general an upright bottle is to be preferred to the boat-shaped type, as it is easier to heat, there are no valves to go wrong, or to clean, and baby swallows less air.

If you decide to make up all your feeds at once, when using fresh milk—you will need five or six bottles. It is nice, too, to have a wire cage in which they can stand, and which can be lifted in and out of a large saucepan or sterilizer. An officially stamped measure will also be needed.

Teats should have a bulb at the top end to give baby a grip; and a flange at the base is useful as they may have to be lifted during the

79

feed to allow entry of air. A too-tight teat discourages, a too-loose one gives baby no jaw exercise and may lead to indigestion. To test the rate of flow, tip the half-full bottle downwards, when drops should form and fall at the rate of about 12 a minute. It is a wise plan to use two teats with each feed, a tight one to start with when baby is fresh and hungry, and a looser one to finish.

A flannel bag to cover the bottle helps to maintain its temperature; and it is also important to have a bowl or saucepan of hot water ready, in which to re-heat the bottle when baby is lifted for wind half-way through the feed—which should last in all about 15 to 20 minutes.

Preparing the Feed
Try to prepare the bottle just before it is to be used. Don't set it warming and then go and do a host of small jobs. Never leave the bottle in the pram, or take it along on an outing just warm, for bacteria soon multiply at such a temperature. Throw away any left-overs, or use them for cooking.

Everything which comes into contact with baby's food must be kept scrupulously clean. The mother should never make the food, or give the bottle, without first washing her hands and nails well. Needless to say, she should never touch any part of the food with her fingers. The heat of the milk, if not tested by a thermometer, must be gauged by pouring a few drops on the wrist, or other sensitive part, and *not* by taking a sip of it. Even if a separate spoon were used for this purpose it is a very inaccurate method; grown-ups are so accustomed to hot food that their palates are not sensitive, and milk at blood-heat (right for baby) would taste too cold to them.

Finally, warmth, cuddling and content are important ingredients of every feeding-time. Baby needs emotional as well as physical nourishment. Bottle-feeding should be as much a partnership as breast-feeding to get the best results, and the busy mother's temptation to prop up the bottle and leave baby to get on with it must be resisted.

Cleaning the Bottle
It is important to prevent any film forming on the inside of bottles or teats, so immediately after use, before removing teat, wash both with cold water. Light and damp are enemies of rubber, so, after cleaning teats inside and out with a little common cooking salt,

it is a good plan to store in a covered jar. Just before use pour boiling water freely over them. Sterilize more thoroughly once

daily. Bottles, after their initial rinsing, should be well washed in hot soapy water, or water to which a little washing-soda has been added. Rinse thoroughly. Use a bottle brush kept for the purpose and boil this frequently.

For sterilizing many mothers like the Milton method, in which bottles and teats are left submerged between feeds. If you use the boiling method, put your bottles and teats in cold water, bring to

the boil, boil steadily for five minutes and leave to cool in a covered container, extracting the teats with a perforated spoon, drying and storing in a dry, dark place.

Bottle-feeding

Most babies will be dieted by their doctor or clinic, and adjustments to suit the individual baby and his stage of development must be made. The following specimen recipes, based on the teaching of the Mothercraft Training Society, are suitable for the average baby of three to three and a half months.

Fresh Milk Mixture (30 oz.)

T.T. Milk	.	16½ oz.
Sugar of milk (lactose) ⎤ .	.	3 tablespoons
or ⎬ .	.	2 tablespoons
Cane Sugar ⎦		+ 1 teaspoon
Water . . . ⎤ .	.	13½ oz.
Govt. oil with buttter . ⎪ .	.	1 teaspoon
or ⎬		+ 2 teaspoons
50 Cod-liver Oil Emulsion, ⎪		
Brestol, or Kariol ⎦ .	.	6 teaspoons

Kariol (obtainable from the M.T.S., 193, Dyke Road, Hove) and Brestol (Cow and Gate) contain 40 per cent. sugar, so if using either of these excellent preparations the amount of sugar in the recipe should be reduced by one-third.

Dried Milk Mixtures (6 oz.)

Full Cream dried milk . .	.	3½ levelled measures
Sugar of milk (lactose) ⎤ .	.	2½ teaspoons
or ⎬		
Cane sugar ⎦ .	.	1¾ teaspoons
Water to	.	6 oz.
Govt. oil + butter ⎤ .	.	1 teaspoon + 2 tea-
or ⎬		spoons (one-fifth
50 per cent. Cod-liver ⎪		portion)
Oil Emulsion . ⎦ .	.	1⅛ teaspoons

Measure the exact amount of fat for the day into a little jar and give a fifth portion at each feed.

Make each feed separately, giving five feeds in the 24 hours.

Directions for Making. Wash hands thoroughly and scald all utensils before using. Keep on an enamel tray. When measuring sugar, or emulsion, use kitchen spoons and level with knife. If milk comes in bottle, pour into a scalded jug and stir well before measuring.

Bottle-feeding

Bring measured quantity of milk, water, and sugar, quickly to the boil, and strain through muslin into a jug.

Or, mix dried milk to a paste, using a little boiling water in which the sugar has been dissolved. Gradually add the remainder of the sugared water, stirring well. Strain.

Stand milk in covered jug in basin, under running water, until quite cold.

Store in a cool place, covered with a piece of wet muslin large enough to allow all four corners to hang in the water.

Heat by standing bottle in jug of hot water.

FOR FURTHER READING

The Mothercraft Manual, by M. Liddiard, C.B.E. (12th edn.), Churchill, 5s.
Babies and Young Children, by R. S. and C. M., Illingworth. Churchill, 18s.

XVIII

EARLY EXTRAS

IF WE LOOK ahead to the first birthday, when we hope baby will be established on a fairly varied solid diet, we can see that the infant has a great deal to learn during his first year. To be gradual is important, so it is best to make an early start in giving extras, so that he may have practise in managing various tastes and textures well before the weaning stage is reached.

The first lesson baby has to learn is to accept the look and feel of new utensils. Instead of a soft teat or nipple he must tolerate a bone, plastic, or silver spoon in his mouth. Later the feel of a rim to his beaker has to be accepted too. Nearly all babies enjoy fruit juice, so the wise mother offers this as the first taste and indeed the modern baby usually is given a little fruit juice as early as two or three weeks of age (see p. 76).

Fruit Juices

As he grows, at three months or so, he can be offered—singly or in combination—blackcurrant, rose-hip, pineapple, raspberry, peach, greengage, cherry juices—almost any fruit juice which does not require sugar to make it palatable. Such fruit should be sieved to hold back any seeds, and tasted before giving. If sugar must be added, a little melted honey or Barbados sugar is better than the refined white sugar, or rose-hip syrup can be used for sweetening purposes. Juices must be well diluted at first; the extra water will be good for baby, and risks of upsets will thus be minimized. One part of juice to six parts of water, gradually increasing the juice and reducing the water to half and half is a good plan.

Baby will also early be given some form of vitamin A and D (see p. 76), introducing another type of food, which fortunately slips down very readily as a rule.

Vegetable Juices

The next extra to introduce is vegetable juices. The great value of these is that they contain a number of minerals, including iron, of which baby stands in special need. The iron stored in his body before birth is running low and milk is not a good source of supply. They are also alkaline in reaction.

Raw vegetable juices are more valuable than cooked ones, but need more careful cleansing. Grate on to clean muslin and squeeze or press ; or cover the grated material with a little water, and stand in a covered cup for two hours.

Learning to Eat
At about four months of age a new stage is reached, for if a little solid food is put on a baby's tongue, he is by now able to transfer it to the back of the mouth and swallow it. This is a new accomplishment, which most babies find enjoyment in practising, if provided with something agreeable with which to do so.

At four months most babies are very mouth-conscious. They champ and chew, blow bubbles and spit, and bite on articles which come their way. This surely is nature's cue to let them have the right material for mouth exercise. A Bickiepeg will probably be enjoyed and give jaw exercise without upsetting the digestion.

Vegetable Purees
Pulps and purees should now replace the juices and these can oftened be thickened with advantage.

The small tins and jars many firms provide for baby-feeding are very useful to the busy mother, but of course she can quite well prepare her own. Choose young and tender vegetables which are in season; clean and dice, or shred, and cook in a little slightly salted water (celery salt is good), with a little added fat to prevent sticking. Use any released juices in broths.

Always taste a vegetable before offering it to baby, for, once his suspicion or antagonism has been aroused, feeding difficulties loom ahead. If the flavour seems too strong, too distinctive, or too dull, it is wise to make additions or adjustments—to add just a little Marmite; or mix in a few breadcrumbs, or a tablespoon of milk, or blend with another vegetable. Potatoes are best cooked in their skins and should be well mashed or sieved.

Start with half teaspoon portions and increase gradually, going back to the small portion with each new vegetable in turn. Baby should be able to deal with about 2 tablespoons at 6–8 months.

Watch the stools, but do not take alarm by changes in colour or traces of undigested material in them if baby is quite happy and free from discomfort. Reduce temporarily if it seems wise.

Fruit pulp should be given once or twice a day. Apples are specially valuable and can be grated and given raw, or stewed, or baked with a little honey and sieved. Bananas, well-ripened, should be sliced down the middle to remove seeds, and mashed across the fibres with a fork. Soaked raisins and figs, sieved at first, and other dried fruits are useful additions to the diet. But practically all fruits in season can be used.

Eggs are a food which provide good nutrients but, because of their great richness, may not be immediately tolerated. Start with half a teaspoon (raw if really fresh), mixed well with a tablespoon of milk, or a little vegetable to begin with. Another plan is to hard boil, powder the yolk well, and give just a little of this. The white should not be introduced until baby has learned to take a whole yolk, and he can only do this by degrees. Coddle the egg so that the white remains creamy (see p. 228). If there seems any upset, leave it for a week, and then try again with a still smaller quantity.

Cereals include a wide range of foods well tolerated and enjoyed by the average baby. It is probably not very wise to introduce them under five months, and the aim must always be not to give in excess, as they tend to make weight without bone.

After baby has learned to deal with a Bickiepeg, it is as well to start each meal with something hard on which he can gnaw and bite, such as home-made rusks, pulled bread, or Chu Chus.

His oats or barley, introduced at six or seven months, can be made into firm jelly form, on which he must mouth; and soft foods, such as sponge cakes or thin bread and butter, should be withheld until the art of mastication has become second nature, preferably until the full set of milk teeth are through.

Prepared cereals (specially suited to the young baby) have their place in providing variety and being labour-saving to the mother. Some can be combined with a thicker cereal or added to vegetable broths. Those with a wheat base are especially good. Work cereals gradually up to about three tablespoons at a year, giving once or twice a day.

Vegetables, fruits, egg yolk, milk, cereals—these are five basic food groups with which we wish baby to become happily familiar. We are all creatures of habit, custom and tradition, and that is why it is important to take real trouble to widen the range of baby's favourites and not to offer him over-sweet, or over-savoury, or over-soft food, which might make him turn from simpler and more worth-while dishes.

Wholesome nutrients, taken in a happy, friendly atmosphere, with plenty of opportunity for exercising the jaws and erupting teeth, will ensure his good, all-round development during the pre-weaning and weaning stages.

FOR FURTHER READING

Your Child and Diet, by Dr. Pink and Helen Rathbone. Blandford Press, 6s.
Feeding Mothers and Babies, by Nell Heaton. Faber & Faber, 7s. 6d.
Simple Guide to Healthy Food, London Health Centre, Wigmore Street, W.1., 1s. + Postage.

XIX

WEANING

'To wean' just means to accustom, and the word is principally used to describe the two big feeding adjustments which every baby must make: (1) learning to deal with solids instead of fluids only; and (2) learning to gulp and swallow, instead of only sucking and swallowing. That is the giving up of baby ways of imbibing food and turning into an independent little one who can manage a cup and spoon, chew and masticate. This chapter deals only with the milk side of the dietary. The solids are considered on p. 94.

Ideally baby takes his main nourishment from the breast for eight to nine months, and ideally he takes at least five weeks to make the change over from breast or bottle, to cup and spoon. Weaning may have to be done much earlier than this in certain cases, and sometimes it must be more sudden, but let us look at the ideal first.

Emotionally, as well as physically, the act of suckling has great significance to a young baby. It is a great comfort to him in times of stress; it satisfies oral impulses, and it develops the soft palate. It is a pity then to cut it too short. At the same time, weaning from suckling to drinking is accomplished more easily before baby becomes too set. Determination grows with age and custom, and the mother who has not begun weaning by the time baby is nine months may find herself in for a struggle.

Some babies ask to be weaned. They appear quite offended when offered liquids and slops, and demand solids. They turn their heads away from breast or bottle, but accept cup or spoon with alacrity. These are in a minority, however; the majority of babies are weaned to suit their mother's convenience rather than their own. They may be highly annoyed in the process, feel deprived, even go on hunger-strike in an attempt to cling to the ways to which they have become happily accustomed.

Weaning

Babies are little individualists, with their moods and ups and downs. Most of them are a bit suspicious of any kind of change and prefer the old paths. Offer a young baby a spoon and, irrespective of what is in it, his first impulse is to use his tongue to eject it. Offer cup instead of breast, and his instinct is to clamp the mouth or turn away. But babies are very teachable, especially if you catch them at the right time, and if you yourself keep smiling and confident.

Feeding Utensils

Baby will need special help to make the new ways enjoyable. Don't let him bury his face in what must seem to him an enormous mug from which a wide torrent of milk flows. The use of an 'Ideal' feeding-cup with a spout, a cream-jug with a projecting lip, or one of the special feeders on the market, will help to avoid his being swamped in more senses than one. Alternatively, an egg-cup or medicine-glass may be tried—something light to hold, and shallow in content, so that spills do not make too much of a mess.

Whatever beaker you use, let the strangeness wear off by allowing some play with it, and if the first contents are of a flavour to which baby is already partial, it will help to overcome suspicions. He enjoys a bright colour too.

If baby sucks his thumb a lot, or tries to suck rather than to drink, it may be he would be better on a bottle for a little longer, or at any rate, for part of each feed. Watch his reactions and treat him as an active partner, not a robot.

If you are weaning in the ninth month baby may be on a five-feed or a four-feed programme. In many ways it is easier if he has the extra feed, so that he does not have too large an amount to tackle at a time, nor go too long if a feed has not been wholly satisfactory.

The First Change

Stage-managing the first cup feeds is important. To put baby more or less into the attitude for nursing and then refuse the breast is really cruel. If someone else can offer the first meals it is best, but if the mother is single-handed she should seek to break the old associations as far as possible. The child should sit up in his high chair, or 'Little Buffer', and this should be near a window, or in a different room from the one in which he is usually nursed. A

Teddy bear may make a friendly, hungry third; a shining silver spoon with short loop-handle, easy for baby fingers, will provide distractions. The use of a mirror often helps, as he sees 'the other fellow' taking his drink just at the same time as himself!

If all the milk is not taken, it is no tragedy. Baby will make up for it at the next feed. If, however, it is refused altogether and baby has but a single thought, to get to the breast, then it is wisest not to prolong the struggle unduly, but to offer solids or a fruit drink which he may accept happily.

It is not wise to give the breast, for if you struggle for a time and then give in, you are encouraging baby to persevere in his refusals next time. If you forcibly feed him, or fuss a great deal over the new food, he will take a dislike to the pleasant cup, and its mere appearance next time may be enough to cause a tantrum.

Remember that your baby is much more 'babyish' and dependent when he first wakes, or when he's getting sleepy. Weaning adjustments should, therefore, start at the 2 p.m. feed, when baby is wide awake and interested, and not unduly ravenous.

The Second Change
Once baby has accepted the pattern of the 2 p.m. feed, and indeed even if he has not fully done so, it is best to go on to the second change, after a week or ten days. Now cup and spoon are offered at 10 a.m. and 6 p.m., the breast being allowed at 2 p.m., which eases the mother. When in a further week or so it is time for the third change, the cup is offered at 10 and 2 and 6—the three day-feeds. Many babies give up the 10 p.m. feed by this stage, and at 6 a.m. they are often quite content to lie awake singing and amusing themselves, so that the mother has not the burden of giving a drinking-teaching lesson too early in the morning. A little drink of fruit juice when she gets up, and an 8 o'clock breakfast,

is usually acceptable. There is, however, no harm in continuing to give the 6 a.m. feed from the breast for another month or so, as long as the supply lasts, if this is the most convenient plan.

The majority of mothers gradually lose their milk as weaning progresses, but a minority find themselves very uncomfortable. Drinking a little less, wearing a firm binder (cutting holes for the nipples), taking a little Epsom or Glauber's salts temporarily may do all that is needed. Express and handle as little as possible, as this stumulates the secretory glands; but do not hesitate to relieve yourself occasionally if in real discomfort. Sponging with hot water will do this for you, or may give baby a short feed.

Summer weaning used to be dreaded in the days when the sterilization of milk and feeding utensils was not fully understood. There are still risks connected with overheating of the system, with dust, flies, etc., but, with care, there is no need to either anticipate or postpone the normal weaning date.

Again, weaning can go on over a holiday if dried milks are used, if there is access to boiling water, and if baby's feeding arrangements can be kept under your own vigilant eye. Breast-fed babies are delightfully easy travellers, but leisurely weaning may make the holiday more enjoyable for the mother.

When is early weaning indicated? This is largely a matter for your doctor, but undoubtedly a great number of babies are weaned prematurely without any due cause and are thus the losers.

The milk 'not suiting'; baby not gaining; the mother feeling tired —none of these are due causes. They can all be put right with intelligent adjustments (see p. 70).

The three main legitimate causes are a further pregnancy; the mother's absence from home because of essential duties; her own rather severe illness, particularly T.B.

Panic measures and drastic changes, throwing a strain on both mother and child, should be avoided whenever it is at all possible, and whenever possible at least a few days be taken over each change —particularly the first two. The milk mixture offered should be suited to baby's age and best given a little weak to begin with.

LEAFLETS AVAILABLE

Early Extras.
First Solids.
How to Wean a Baby from 7–9 *Months.*
Milk Mixtures from 6 *Months*, from 'The Woman's Pictorial', The
   Fleetway House, London, E.C.4, a penny each or 2½*d.* by post.

RECIPES FOR WEANING A NORMAL BABY OF SEVEN TO NINE MONTHS
ON TO A FRESH OR DRIED MILK MIXTURE

Take one week over each change	*First week* Artificial Feed 2 p.m.	*Second week* Artificial Feeds 7 oz. at 10 a.m., 6 p.m.	*Third week* Artificial Feeds 7 oz. at 10 a.m., 2 p.m., 6 p.m.	*Fourth week* Artificial Feeds 7 oz. at 10 a.m., 2 p.m., 6 p.m., 10 p.m.	*Fifth week* 4–5 feeds of 7–7½ oz. milk mixture
Fresh milk	3½ oz.	10 oz.	15 oz.	21 oz.	25 oz.
Dried milk (full cream)	3½ measures	10 measures	16 measures	22½ measures	26 measures
Sugar	1½ teas.	3 teas.	1 tabs.	1 tabs. + 2 teas.	1 tabs.
Water to make	7 oz.	14 oz.	21 oz.	28 oz.	30–35 oz.
Cod-liver Oil Emulsion	1 teas.	3 teas.	4 teas.	5 teas.	4 teas.
Government Cod-liver Oil *and* Butter	½ teas. —	1 teas.	1 teas. and 1½ teas.	1 teas. and 1½ teas.	1 teas. and 2 teas.

Tabs. = tablespoon (level)
Teas. = teaspoon (level).

Based on the teaching of the Mothercraft Training Society adapted from the *Mothercraft Manual*, by M. Liddiard. Churchill, 5s.

93

XX

FOOD FOR THE OLDER CHILD

NUTRITION IS A big subject and some mothers shy away from it altogether, just letting the children have what's going. Would a farmer feed his prize stock in this casual fashion? Or a master-builder take so little interest in the type of bricks used in an important building? And the cells of our bodies are built up by our daily food.

It is of course possible to go to the other extreme and become obsessed by diet, turning into a food faddist. Instead of enjoying their food such folk worry about it. If they know some food is good they tend to turn it into a sort of fetish, losing all sense of proportion and often of nutritional balance.

The myriad cells of which our bones and flesh are made up need for their perfect functioning three things—oxygen, fluid and food. If the food they receive is going to really nourish it must be well assimilated, which includes enjoying it, chewing and masticating it, and passing on the waste products formed during its digestion. It must also be chosen wisely, and be sufficiently varied to enable the system to select the particular elements of which it stands in special need.

The Child's Choice.

But while we should try and make a variety of foods attractive to children, yet we must beware of too much adult pressure at any time over the choice of food. Nothing mars a natural appetite more quickly than to have food forced in any way, while tensions and anxieties on the mother's part will have a similar affect. From early days a child should be

94

allowed to feed himself no matter how messy the result at first. Portions should be small, and set out individually, not in a mixture, and the child allowed to make his own selection within reason.

Food Divisions

Food can be roughly divided into three classes—the protective, the body-building and the energy-giving. Alas, there is a fourth class which can only earn the name of 'deficiency' foods.

The protective foods are principally those which are 'whole', that is they have not been refined in ways which mean a loss of minerals; raw, so that they are charged with light, the great source of energy; and those particularly rich in one or other of the vitamins, or life-giving elements the human body needs.

The body-builders are the proteins, and these also see to repair of tissues and maintenance of organs.

The fuel foods—to give heat and energy—are the fats, sugars and starches (carbohydrates). Many items of food are compound, belonging to more than one class, and naturally those which protect, as well as energize or build, are specially valuable.

The 'deficiency' foods, to which reference has been made, are those which have been so processed, adulterated or over-cooked that they have little nourishing property left. They are deficient in vitamins and in minerals, so that the body, in breaking them down, calls on its own mineral reserves, and thus they deplete rather than supply it with nutriment. Many of these foods are cheap, easy to prepare, and quite palatable, and filling the stomach with them serves to blunt the appetite. They include white sugar and white flour and things made with them; shop jams, biscuits and cakes; white rice, sago and tapioca puddings, cornflours and blancmanges, cheap sweets; vegetables thickly peeled, cooked with soda, or overcooked and the water thrown away. Foods of this character should play a very small part in the diet of growing children.

Protein

The protein foods, to be taken every day, include milk, eggs, meat, fish, nuts, cheese, peas, beans and lentils; wholemeal bread and the wheat embryo are other useful sources.

There is more than one school of thought about the amounts of protein needed by children and the best types to supply. There are those who believe in 'rosebud food for rosebud flesh'. They feel that animal protein, and especially meat, is likely to increase purins and toxins in the system. They point to the over-stimulating properties of meat; its acid reaction in digestion; the tax on liver and kidneys which it imposes. Vegetarians, lacto-vegetarians and fruitarians can all point to sturdy and beautiful specimens of childhood reared on meatless menus.

Others believe that it is best not to be in too great a hurry to introduce meat, partly on account of its waste products, and partly because it may spoil the palate for less savoury but yet important dishes, and would withhold for say 18 months.

On the other hand, there are those who would start meat very young indeed, who would so pound and mice it that it can be given long before the teeth erupt, and who believe that it alone can earn the name of being a first-class protein.

Those who seek to follow a middle pathway will probably wish to start meat at about a year and give it some two or three times a week. They will choose chicken, rabbit, lamb and sweetbreads at first in preference to mutton and beef, and eschew veal and pork altogether.

Fish is an alternative source of protein, and some kinds are more readily digested than meat. It provides iodine, phosphorus and calcium, and, in the case of fatty fish, vitamins A and D. (The calcium is found principally in the tiny bones.) Start at about eight to nine months with a very tender lean fish, such as sole or plaice, or hake, steam in a little milk, and then flake. Herrings have a high nutritive value but great care must be taken over the little bones. Give fish some three times a week.

Cheese is a valuable food because it is a rich source of calcium. Soft cheese can be digested from about eight to nine months, in small quantities. They can be home-made very simply—see p. 227. Later a mild, harder cheese can be flaked, left to dry for a few hours, and then used with vegetables or broths. At a year, slices can be taken in the fingers and eaten in this way.

Eggs, if well tolerated can be given three times a week with advantage. The yolk is rich in phosphorous and iron and in the fat soluble vitamins A and D, and the white comprises a useful protein.

Nuts are most usually given in the form of a cream, or milk, the almond being particularly good. If the mother has a nut-mill she can combine a sprinkling of nuts with dates or raisins to make a nourishing dish.

Pulses can be used in soups and in simple baked dishes, combined with egg or cheese. The protein thus provided is more economical than that derived from meat, but equally good for the growing body. In pastes and powders, pulses can be introduced after six months.

All animal proteins are acid in reaction, hence it is important always to combine with vegetables, which leave an alkaline residue after digestion.

Fuel Foods

Fuel foods are of two kinds—*fats* and *carbohydrates*. Fats which contain also the protective vitamins A and D include halibut and cod-liver oil, cream, butter from cows out to grass, cheese ditto, fortified margarine, herrings, sardines, kidneys and liver.

The best carbohydrates are those which are whole, not processed or refined, and these contain Vitamin B—whole wheat, oat, barley, and rice; and a 100 per cent wholemeal loaf made from stoneground, and, if possible, compost-grown flour. Roughage must of course be excluded until the child's digestion is more mature. Dark brown sugar, black treacle, good honey, are valuable energizers rich in natural minerals.

Breakfast

Breakfast round about 8 a.m. should start with fruit whenever possible, fresh or dried. This should be combined with milk, and can be fortified with cereals such as corn flakes, Wheetabix, Grape Nuts, Frugrains, Bemax, etc., or raw oatmeal made into a Muesli (see p. 228). Wholemeal toast, or crispbreads, with butter or margarine, honey or black treacle, can follow. The use of a little peanut butter or almond cream with the toast gives extra nourishment. When school-days are reached, a cooked dish is usually needed to fortify the child for an energetic morning. This can be egg, bacon, fish, etc., if wished.

If a child is off colour at any time, give fruit and milk only at breakfast for a few days to lighten the digestive load, and to ensure a better appetite for the important midday meal.

The Midday Meal

Dinner is the time when a good protein dish is essential. It should

97

be combined with raw and cooked vegetables. Try and serve one root and one leafy vegetable, as well as potato, with meat or fish. Lettuce with grated carrot, diced apple, grated cheese, raisins, etc., is often popular. A thick vegetable broth, made by dicing a number of vegetables, with the addition of a little pea flour or some lentils, is a healthy first course, especially if the protein dish to follow is light.

A pudding course is not necessary for the first 15 months or so, the child finishing with a little drink of milk. After that, it can take the form of baked apple, fruit salad, baked custard, or a steamed pudding, etc.

Tea-Supper

A tea-supper meal about 5.15 is ideal for the first five years, after which it is best to give a tea about four, followed by a light supper half an hour before bedtime.

At one or other give a simple protein dish: e.g. poached or scrambled egg, savoury baked potatoes, herring or cod roes, sardines, a thickened vegetable broth, etc; with some salad material, such as watercress, shredded cabbage, beet, tomatoes, etc; good brown crusty bread, with Marmite or other yeast extract, a piece of home-made cake or parkin occasionally, and milk or malted milk to drink.

Supper

If the pre-school child needs anything before bed a cup of vegetable broth is best. Nothing that can cling to the teeth or disturb the digestion should be offered. It is a good plan to try to end every meal with something which sets the salivary glands working, and tends to clean the teeth. A piece of apple is ideal, but a hard rusk or clean carrot will do.

Fluids

Do not forgot the importance of water. It has been called the very fount of nutrition. A child is composed of nearly 70 per cent water. All his body cells are surrounded by nutrient fluid, on the proper composition of which depends their vitality. Fortunately the majority of foods include a great deal of water, and this is especially so with fruits, vegetables and milk. While we do not want to press a child to drink, it is wise to make water readily available. If he forms the habit of taking a drink an hour before a meal it will be healthy for him. It is also a useful health habit to take a drink of water first thing in the morning.

FOR FURTHER READING

Children's Diet Sheet, from 'The Woman's Pictorial', The Fleetway
    House, London, E.C.4, 2½d. by post.
Care of Children from 1–5 *Years*, by J. Gibbens. Churchill, 5s.
Good Food for Growing Children, from the London Health Centre,
    9, Wigmore Street, London, W.1, 6d. plus postage.

XXI

BABY'S DAY

WHEN BABY WAKES in the morning round about 6 a.m. he will be very wet. He will also be very hungry. The wise mother will have put ready over-night everything likely to be needed for the first feed, including two well-aired (and covered) napkins. If the weather is cold, she will switch on some heat before picking baby up, to change and make comfortable. She will then put him down for a minute or two, to enable her to wash her hands well, and dry them thoroughly, before swabbing the breasts, or warming the bottle.

After the feed, baby is given an opportunity to relieve himself, and then put down warm and dry, either in an airy room by himself, or, in fine weather, out-of-doors.

Baby will probably sleep, or drowse, again until 9 a.m. and meanwhile the mother can dress, see to breakfast and household chores, and start collecting everything needed for the bath. If baby is bottle-fed she will make the feeds and sterilize equipment at this time (see p. 79). The perambulator must also be got ready, being sure that everything in it is well aired, and kept covered from damp air.

The bath (see p. 63) can start about 9.40 a.m., giving baby opportunity for kicking exercise, and his drink of orange juice, before he goes into it. The 10 o'clock feed over, baby is tucked up for his outdoor rest, and the mother should then make a point of putting her feet up for a quarter of an hour, sipping a nourishing drink, looking at the paper, or in other ways relaxing before she tackles household tasks. Nappy washing, laundering baby garments, and preparation of boiled water and fruit drinks, must be fitted in before her lunch—which should be taken not later than 12.45, so that she is less likely to be disturbed during it by baby demanding attention.

Out-of-Doors
In settling baby in the pram, attention to the position of the sun and

the direction of the wind should be noted, and natural shade sought when possible. A cat net may be needed. When baby wakens, as he gets more active, it is a good plan to put a roll of blanket at the foot of the pram, tucking the top cover over this, so that its weight is lifted off baby's feet and yet he keeps warm. When he gets to the

sitting-up stage the middle leather cushion should be removed after his sleep, so that his feet can go down into the well.

Ten minutes before his next feed is due (or half an hour or so beforehand when he is older) lift baby from the pram for a little mothering, exercise and change of position, to promote good appetite for the meal and ensure drowsiness after it.

The Afternoon

The 2 p.m. feed over, baby will be ready for an afternoon sleep, or quiet time, and mother can lie down and relax thoroughly for an hour. Baby will not need taking for a walk until he is at least six months old, but unless she has someone with whom to leave him, she may sometimes have to take him with her to the shops, though ideally she will keep him away from contact with crowds—his resistance to infections is very low at first.

Mother should have an early cup of tea so that by 4.30 p.m. she is ready to give baby her undivided attention. Let him have his water or fruit juice and then (after he is two months old) put him on a clean rug in play-pen or draught-proof corner—not in front of a fire, which draws draughts to it. If the mother stays on the rug and talks to him for a little while he will accept the new position without fear. While he is little he needs turning over on to his tummy for part of the time, and he must be picked up just as soon as he shows signs of fatigue. The floor freedom is better for the spine than kicking on the lap and is part of his education. The second half of baby's play time should be passed in his mother's arms, and as he grows he will enjoy being carried around to look out of the window, listening to quiet music, playing with some teething peg, etc.

Bedtime

At 5.30 baby has his day garments removed, is topped and then tailed, put into his aired night garments, given his evening feed, and is tucked up warm and dry for the night.

Mother then has a good clear up, collects what is needed for the morning, and is free to devote herself to Daddy and his needs for

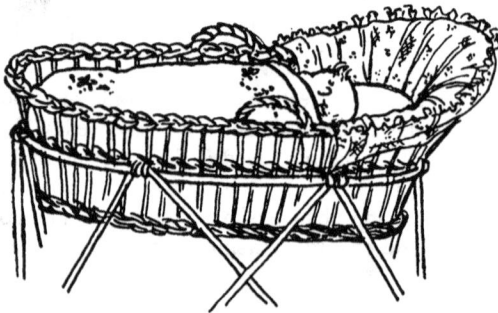

the rest of the time. If Daddy will bring baby to mother in bed for the ten o'clock feed it ensures that she has as long a night as possible. Daddy will soon become expert in handling his baby at this time, and will not forget to bring up wind specially well, so that the risk of being disturbed in the night is diminished.

The very young baby cannot always manage without a night feed, and for the first weeks, should he wake, it is best to give a small feed rather than to let him cry in a worried, lonely, hungry way and disturb the whole household. He will drop this of his own accord as he gets a little older and if care is taken to see that the last two feeds are satisfactory ones.

PLAN OF BABY'S DAY

6 a.m. Baby's first feed; hold out; change and put back into cot to sleep.

8 a.m. Mother's breakfast, necessary housework, etc. Get everything ready for baby's bath. If artificially fed, milk mixture to be made for the 24 hours, ready for the 10 o'clock feed.

9.45 a.m. Bath, dress and feed baby. Hold out. (This will take about 1 hour.)

10.45 a.m. Put to sleep in cot or pram, in garden or by open window.

2 p.m. Feed and hold out. If awake early, can have kicking time on mother's lap about 20 minutes before the feed—later in pen or on the floor. Back into cot or pram in garden or take out for a walk (not necessary during the first six months). Mother should try and get at least half-hour's rest with her feet up sometime during the afternoon.

4 p.m.–4.30 p.m. If awake can have a drink of water, or orange juice, if artificially fed.

5 p.m.–6 p.m. Mothering time, undressed and evening toilet done.

6 p.m. Feed, hold out, and put in cot.

10 p.m. Baby's last feed. If possible, mother should get ready for bed before giving feed, in order to get a long night's sleep herself.

ROUTINE FOR THE ONE TO TWO-YEAR-OLD

6.30–7 a.m. When awake change; hold out; sit up with dressing-gown on and a toy to play with. Give a raw apple and drink of water or fruit juice.

8 a.m. Cold sponge and dress, and allow crawling or toddling exercise.

8.30–9 a.m. Breakfast: sit out; allow to play outside and then to sit in pram. Later, romping about in the garden may be allowed.

10.45 a.m. Orange juice and water to drink; tuck in for morning sleep.

12.30–1 p.m.   Give a drink of water; sponge hands and face; short playtime before dinner. Dinner; toilet; rest in pram; then allow exercise outside.

2.15 p.m.   Get ready for afternoon outing in pram. After 15 months toddler may walk a little when out.

4.15 p.m.   Drink of fruit juice in water.

4.45–5.15 p.m.   Tea-supper.

5.15 p.m.   Playtime and Mothering time.

6 p.m.   Bath and put into bed.

10 p.m.   Lift, make comfortable for night.

SUNBATHING

The virtues of sunbathing are rightly extolled, but sometimes it is forgotten how powerful are the rays the sun emits, and thus what care is needed if summer sunshine is to do the maximum of good with the minimum of risk.

If possible sunbathing should begin round about April 1st with any baby older than three months, and be carried on steadily throughout the year until the late autumn. Even when the sky is overcast a daily air-bath should be taken, for many beneficial rays in the atmosphere will be absorbed. In very hot weather, sunlight filtered through foliage is safer than a direct exposure.

Start by exposing arms and legs only for two to three minutes. Increase the time by a minute each day up to, say, ten minutes. If winds are keen the infant should be just inside a widely-open window, or in the perambulator, being careful to see that he does not face a glare. Always turn a pram or cot so that baby's feet point towards the sun, and brow and eyelids shield the sensitive eyes— remembering that the sun keeps moving! If necessary a light linen hat, with a brim back and front, can be worn. After a few days the child's front can be exposed, starting with a short period, working up to ten minutes or so; then treat the back in a similar fashion. Soon baby will be enjoying a 20 minute sun-bathe with no clothing, apart perhaps for a thin napkin. If a reasonable area of the skin receives the ultra-violet rays the whole system benefits, thus there is no particular value in being quite naked, while the area of groin and thighs is particularly sensitive to sunburn.

The toddler, or older child, whose skin has been muffled with clothes throughout the winter, needs a gradual re-education in the same way, and the fairer the skin, the more precaution must be taken. Normally the action of sunlight activates the pigment-making cells and soon brings about a protective tanning. This reaction must be a very much slower process with those with little pigment in the skin tissues. Therefore, when the sun is strong, such children should always wear some covering, to include arms and ankles, to prevent the too-free penetration of powerful rays which might

cause inflammation or burns. Alternatively, the skin can be covered well with protective oils. Such precaution, while wise, in itself does not teach a progressive tolerance to light. This must not be neglected, though such training must be extremely gradual.

In the same way if a child's eyes seem weak, to let him wear dark glasses will temporarily ease the situation, but will also tend to perpetuate it. Good light, but not glare, should reach children's eyes freely and, in time, will strengthen them.

Heat Stroke

In this country the sun's rays are rarely powerful enough to make the wearing of a hat an essential for any child with a fairly good thatch of hair and pigmented skin. The so-called 'sun stroke' which may occur is more accurately 'heat stroke'. When the air is very still, if the child is very energetic, the body may not be able to lose enough heat to maintain its normal equilibrium. So in a heat-wave great care must be taken to avoid any such possibility. Thirty minutes play in the direct sun is quite long enough for most children—unless they are playing with water, which has a cooling effect. After this shade should be sought. This is important, especially in open fields or parks, or on a beach, where the sun's rays are very powerful, and between 11 a.m. and 4 p.m. when the sun is strongest.

If a child does a lot of perspiring it is not enough to give him plenty of fluid—though he needs this. He also needs to replace the salt which he is losing through his skin. A teaspoon of salt to a pint of water, or lemonade, will put things right for him. Otherwise he may suffer from a form of cramp.

Sunburn

Always be on the look out for any signs of reddening of the skin, but do not forget that the reaction of the body to the sun's warmth will go on long after the exposure is ended, and a resulting ache, pain, or burn, may not show itself for some hours. Hence the importance of really making haste slowly, and rationing the sunlight much as you ration cod-liver oil, or any other good thing.

After a sunbath it is good to rub the skin down very well because of body poisons which will have come to the surface. If your child has a naturally dry skin, finish with rubbing in a little oil or cream.

Laying in a store of sunshine through the summer helps the system to fight the infections rife in the winter-time. Sunshine makes for happiness, contentment, vitality and good growth. It is only when an overdose is allowed that its effects may be adverse.

FOR FURTHER READING

The Nursery Years, by Susan Isaacs. Routledge, 3s. 6d. (cloth), 2s. 6d. (paper).

The Care of Young Babies, by Dr. John Gibbens. Churchill, 5s.

The Commonsense Book of Child and Baby Care, by Benjamin Spock. Dent, 10s. 6d., 4s. (paper covers).

XXII

CRYING

SMALL PERIODS OF crying, even up to a dozen in a day, are quite
normal in a young baby. It is the only way he can tell you his needs
and, at least until the lungs are fully stretched—say for the first
fortnight—he needs to cry to give them exercise. But what if he
cries on and on? If his crying increases rather than lessens when he
should be settling down?

A well-known maternity home recently conducted an interesting
experiment. The actual crying done by a group of normally cared-
for babies was carefully recorded. It came to two and a half hours
a day. Then extra special care and attention was given to the
same group and crying was gradually reduced to only one hour a
day.

Why does a baby cry? The answer in nine cases out of ten is
because he isn't comfortable. Is this his fault? Surely not. Baby is
quite helpless and dependent on the ministrations he receives. It
is a mistake then always to attribute crying to naughtiness, or to
suggest that 'as he's got to learn he can't have or do this or that',
he shouldn't be comforted. (There is a place for firmness but it
comes only after all needs have been adequately met.)

What baby needs to learn first of all is that the world is a safe,
secure and happy place, for it is only on such a foundation that
later training can be wisely based.

Hunger and Overfeeding

Discomforts that trouble infants come primarily from the tummy.
It may be empty. Hunger really hurts a baby, and as he is quite free
from inhibitions, or stiff upper lips, he naturally protests as loudly
as he can. When the stomach is empty, cramp-like contractions
occur; while if there is wind in the intestines, there will be **spasms**
of its muscular wall too.

Crying

Overfeeding, which often occurs in the early weeks, leads to rather similar symptoms while the digestive tract is immature.

The baby with 'colic'—which may spring from under- or over-feeding—will draw up his legs, arch his back, go red in the face and 'scream the house down'. Should his mother seek to soothe the trouble by a feed or not?

The stools provide one clue. Too loose and frequent often suggest the milk has been taken too fast. Too frothy, that there is too much sugar in the bottle, or the mother's diet, or in any fruit juice given. Too curdy, that fats or proteins may be in excess.

Weight is another pointer. Normally, baby loses a certain puffiness during the first days, so that, even if he gains as much as an ounce a day, he's not likely to regain his birth-weight under 10 days. After this he should put on six, seven, or eight ounces a week (the lighter baby should gain more rapidly than the heavier one). Over-rapid gain may seem encouraging, but, cumulatively, it may over-strain digestive organs. On slow gains some babies look bright and happy, but because they are underfed, they are not building up their tissues as well and strongly as they should.

Put together the type of stool, the type of gain, the type of cry, the probable rate of suction, and you'll get a fairly good idea whether over- or under-feeding is waking your child. Then matters can be set right intelligently.

Discomforts

Apart from digestive troubles, baby may cry because he's either too hot or too cold. He was beautifully warm in the womb, but not uncomfortably hot. Cold feet and a chilly feeling generally make him unhappy: too many clothes make him stuffy and interfere with his breathing, so he cries for more air.

Unsympathetic handling, loud voices, hard mattresses, harsh clothes next to the skin, or any other discomfort, such as a wet or tight nappy, or a badly placed pin, makes baby tense, fearful, and out of ease.

Then there is loneliness. He was never lonely in the womb. He can feel intensely alone in a large room. Baby needs frequent reassurance, frequent close contact—warmth, softness, cuddling. He may be anxious, too, for his emotions are very early involved in the processes of learning and growing.

Crying

Loving and understanding mothering gives baby a feeling o
security and calm, which helps him to digest his food and to fall
soundly asleep with literally nothing to cry for.

Sickness

A further reason for crying is that he may be feeling poorly or be
sickening for something. One of the most usual of such troubles is
caused by picking up a family cold (see p. 214). Babies are born
natural nose-breathers, and when the little nose is blocked they are
in great discomfort. Always see the nose is clear before feeds.

As the brain develops and the crying reflex—entirely automatic
at first—begins to come under some measure of control, crying for
such things as hunger, thirst, or wet napkins, will decrease, and
baby will be able to lie awake for quite a time before demanding
to be fed or changed.

The Older Baby

Fresh causes of crying occur, however, as the personality develops,
round about 6 months. Fear of strange places and strange faces, for
instance. Denial of opportunities of practising new skills, or the
sudden ending of a happy pleasurable experience, may all lead to
crying as the child takes a greater interest in activities of all kinds.
The baby who won't be good in his pram is perhaps longing to sit
up and look around. The one who cries when his napkin is changed,
dislikes the helpless feeling of being put on his back. The one who
weeps when he comes out of the bath is feeling frustrated in his
desires.

Mother wit is needed to make sensible adjustments, satisfying
to the continuously developing child. If a treat must be cut short,
some happy alternative can be offered, with which to distract his
attention and, let us hope, win his joyous co-operation for 'what
comes next.'

There may, of course, be times when it is best to ignore a baby or
older child when he is crying for an attention which would not be
in his best interests. But, before you decide he's merely 'trying it
on', consider life from his point of view sympathetically and remember that to satisfy is not the same as to spoil.

FOR FURTHER READING

Children's Fears and Jealousies, from the N.A.M.H., 39, Queen Anne
  Street, London, W.1, 1s. 4½d.
Temper Tantrums, from the N.A.M.H., 1s. 4½d.
Disturbed Sleep, by Flora Shepherd. Edwin Payne, Hatfield, Herts. 2s.

XXIII

SLEEP

QUIET SLEEP IS very important to baby, and to the household where he lives. It is normal for him at first to wake only for his feeds, or when in discomfort. That is he should—and usually does—sleep some 20–21 hours out of the 24.

During the early months growth is extremely rapid, especially of the delicate brain. It is during sleep that most of that growth takes place, that tissues are renewed, cell batteries recharged, and the nervous and other systems strengthened, so it is understandable that the more growing there is to be done, the more prolonged must sleep be. As the rate of growth steadies down, after the first six months, baby can afford to lie awake for longer; 18 hours' sleep is ample now. Day naps continue to gradually shorten themselves until, by about three years, as a rule, none is needed, though it is a good plan to continue to arrange for a rest off the feet towards the middle of the day. A long night of 11–12 hours is essential throughout childhood.

Wakefulness
When this refreshing, body-building sleep is constantly interrupted we must ask ourselves what is going wrong, and not be content to consider baby as 'naughty', nor his conduct as something 'only to be expected'. In the early days elusive sleep nearly always has a digestive origin. The tired system is unable to defend itself, and windy pains and fidgetty feelings, associated with indigestion, set baby crying when he should be sleeping.

Remove any such causes of wakefulness, and others discussed on p. 108, and the young baby inevitably falls soundly asleep; it is not until round about the ninth month that he will begin to try to keep himself awake.

In training a young baby to good sleep-habits it is best not to talk to or play with him just after a feed. He may be very attractive then,

Sleep

full, and content, but that is really the time to gently settle him—on his side or tummy and not on his back—so that he slips into dreamless slumber as quickly as possible. If he wakes in between feeding-hours, the attentions given to him should be quiet, and just enough to comfort, but not to stimulate and arouse more thoroughly.

At night in the early days, while the mother is convalescing, it is wise to have baby's cot accessible to her bed, but on the window side of it. Often if she puts out her hand gently she can reassure a startled or half-aroused baby and send him off to sleep again. After the first few weeks it will be much better for him to sleep alone, and for mother to go to his room to feed him, and not bring him where there are bright lights and other disturbances.

It is a mistake to make a habit of rocking or singing a baby to sleep; getting him to sleep before he is put down; lying down by him, holding his hand, and so on. Children soon become creatures of habit, and without these time-consuming rituals find they cannot get off to sleep. Of course, occasionally to give extra comfort of this kind will do no harm, but if the day has been well-planned, sleep should come quite naturally.

THE TODDLER AND OLDER CHILD

When baby is old enough to pull himself to his feet, he will often fight against being tucked up. The wise mother puts him in a warm dressing-gown and allows him to jump around unrestrained, or controlled by a soft webbing safety-harness. He may take 15–20 minutes before he is relaxed and drowsy, and he may fall asleep in a funny little heap, but it is then quite easy to tuck him up without disturbing him. Whereas, had there been insistence on his lying down, there might have been tears and tensions, making sleep—which is a state of relaxation—impossible.

If a child wakes in the night, and talks or sings to himself, it is usually best to take no notice whatever. If, however, he wakes crying, this is another matter. He may be hungry, or he may have a pain or be frightened. For further discussion of these facts, see p. 201.

Under few, if any, circumstances should a child be taken into his mother's bed; nor should he ever be carried downstairs again after he has once been put to bed. These 'rewards' for crying are likely to perpetuate the trouble as well as over-stimulating the little brain.

As the child becomes more conscious of himself as a person, he often goes through a stage of fighting against sleep, or waking from it with a start, fearful of separation from his mother. These disturbances are particularly marked from about fifteen months to two and a half years. They are best met by extra mothering to fill the last waking moments with happy thoughts, and by going quickly to the child as soon as he stirs, to reassure him. If he keeps calling out for a drink, or attention of some kind, the wise mother stays quietly in his room with her knitting or sewing, to give him the comfort of her presence as he makes the transition from day to night, comforting herself that this is a phase which will pass.

A night light, or the use of 5-watt blue electric bulb, is often appreciated by the nervous child, adept at collecting material for night terrors. Parents must be particularly careful in censoring pictures, stories and scraps of talk in the early years when fantasy life is strong. The underlying fear, however, is nearly always of a broken relationship with the parent, on which the nervy, clinging child depends so specially.

Crying it out

Should a child ever be allowed to 'cry it out'? Yes, there may be occasions when this is the kindest thing to do, if the child is quite definitely 'playing his mother up'. But such training will be of no value if he really has something to cry for—some physical or emotional need unmet, some true fear and anxiety. In any case a time limit should be set to the crying and the child not allowed to become exhausted or hysterical. When a wakeful toddler must be left the mother should explain quite clearly that, while she is going down, perhaps to get Daddy's supper, she won't be far away and the child will be perfectly safe. She should leave the door open and not appear apprehensive or annoyed. Her own calmness and confidence that sleep will soon come will help the child more than any crossness; a good-night prayer and simple blessing quiets and comforts the older child.

Early Waking

Most mothers know what it is to experience 'that sinking feeling' when, only half awake, a cheerful small voice is heard demanding attention of one sort or another—so obviously pleased that it is morning, while she is firmly convinced it is really still night.

Keeping up the child later over-night is a solution often essayed. The objections to this plan seem twofold—that the child uses his vitality at the wrong end of the day and often becomes nervy and troublesome. And that the peace of the home is largely lost, evening quiet and freedom from the care of the child being very necessary to the health and happiness of the parents.

If the toddler wakes early, he should, as soon as he is capable, be encouraged to put on his dressing-gown, and to attend as far as possible to himself. Any conversation that may be necessary being carried on in whispers, to help him to realize it is not yet day.

A few absorbing toys should be at hand, and perhaps a rusk. A contented child will often amuse himself, quite happily talking to the birds, and singing little songs for an hour or more. The demands on his patience are not too great, and the day starts without a sense of rush, if the wise mother gets up at about 7 a.m.

The Day Nap

The question of continuing the day-rest when the child starts protesting against it must be considered. Although children vary, the average child, up to the age of six in particular, benefits from a period off his feet to make a break in a strenuous day. Tiredness will not always show itself in yawning or rubbing the eyes, but rather in a restless excitability, or irritability, clumsiness, or loss of appetite.

Whenever possible a day-rest should be taken out-of-doors and a calming down process should precede it; something enjoyed, such as an apple or orange being given just before the tucking up.

Some children rest better it they are allowed to be in company. The mother may be able to arrange to put her feet up, write letters, or knit, within sight at the resting time. In any case plan to avoid the child feeling banished, or that he is missing something, so that instead of relaxing he is kept on edge.

Before school age, the best time for a rest is before the midday meal, so that the afternoon is clear for adventure, exercise, and fresh air, and the child adequately tired when the 6 o'clock bedtime comes round.

After four years he is old enough to learn how to relax as a game —a useful lesson. Choose some soft toy, and demonstrate how lazily it collapses and flops, suggesting that he does the same. A kitten sets a good example too!

Sleep

Summer Evenings

What about staying up late on summer evenings? Here we must balance the charm of the early-morning hours against that of the golden evenings. The child still needs his long night, and if he settles late may be abed long after the sun is up, and the birds singing around him. An extra half-hour's grace is a useful compromise, and Venetian blinds, or dark curtains may help by cutting off some of the stimulation of the outside light. If baby can sleep outside until the 10 p.m. feed it will be splendid.

A little table giving the more usual hours of sleep is given here, but babies are individuals and the quality of the sleep is as important as its length. A long undisturbed night is of greater value than the same length of sleep taken in shorter stretches. If baby tosses and turns, or sleeps on his tummy, his sleep will not refresh in the same way as if he is thoroughly relaxed and at peace.

Suggested Sleep Requirements

Age	Hours of Sleep	
1 month	21	hours
6 months	18	,,
1 year	15	,,
2 years	13½–14	,,
4 ,,	12½–13	,,
6 ,,	12	,,
9 ,,	11	,,

XXIV

EXERCISE

HAVE YOU EVER stopped to ask yourself why a little child is never still when awake, why a young baby is constantly waving his arms, opening and shutting his hands, threshing with his legs, and straining to raise his head?

The answer is that Nature wants all the tiny fibres of which the immature muscles are formed, the soft cartilages of the unfinished bones, and the internal organs to grow and develop, becoming strong and resilient. Baby's movements give the nerve centres the gentle stimulation they need, improve the circulation, strengthen the heart, set the digestive secretions flowing, enable the lungs to take in more oxygen, and generally do him an immense amount of good.

Without this exercise he would remain weak and flabby, lack tone and vigour, and growth would be seriously hindered.

Is Nature's prompting enough? Ought we to interfere in any way? The answer is both yes and no. Just as an unspoilt appetite is a pretty good guide to the amount of food a baby needs, and yet his mother has to use her native wit in offering the best type of nourishment; so, while baby exercises gamely enough, yet his mother can help him in many ways, especially by giving him freedom to kick at the time of day when his vitality is high and he can respond happily.

Arms and legs will usually get all the work they need, but not the body and head, unless the mother is alert to provide floor space, to

 put baby on his tummy so that he can practise the use of the neck muscles and the first movements of drawing up the legs prior to learning to crawl. The change from sitting and kneeling to

standing and walking is a big one and should be bridged by a fairly
prolonged period on all-fours, by means of which the weight that
the various joints have to bear is evenly distributed.

Rolling is important—it gives massage to the skin, develops the
lungs, brings shoulder and hips into play. It also causes the heart to
beat a little faster—good for that immature organ in moderation—
and tones a sluggish liver.

If you have a rather passive baby it may be wise to give the gentle
stimulation of removing clothes, stroking the little body lightly,
putting a toy just out of reach, etc., so stirring the child to spontaneous action.

Dandling

Do realize that all the muscles want exercise. Dandling the child,
letting him fall back off the lap so that he seeks to pull himself up;
holding him by the ankles upside-down for a few minutes; playing
wheelbarrow as the arms get stronger—are the sort of movements
which, done with discretion and with the child's full enjoyment,
bring chest, back and pelvic muscles into play in a splendid
way.

Baby's own efforts to sit up are educative and gymnastic, too, and
the mother should not immediately come to his aid with a pillow,
though, of course, he will appreciate the support of one for part of
the waking time.

About times: Exercise may not always be enjoyed before a meal if
baby is unduly hungry; it must not be practised strenuously after
one or it would disturb the work of the digestion. It can often be
taken at orange juice time, just before the bath, at mothering time,
and so on; always stopping short of fatigue, and avoiding over-
excitement.

Apart from the physical value of good muscle control, there is,
of course, the effect on character.

The strong, well-developed child solves many of his own problems, becomes independent early, finds he can keep pace with his
friends—life is richer for him, he is likely to be more courageous,
more content. A flabby, lazy body may mean a flabby, lazy mind.

So don't muffle your child with shawls or keep him pram and cot-
bound. As he becomes active, give him scope to explore and roam,
to climb and handle.

Learning to Climb

When he wants to climb the stairs he should be allowed to do so, showing him how to come down backwards in safety. When he wants to explore the house, he should not be kept in his play-pen but given floor freedom. He should be shown how to gauge the height of a table, or to ne-gotiate an edge so as to avoid bumps and bangs. When he longs to climb chairs and tables it can be allowed at suitable times, or substitutes be provided. A safety-gate at the top of the

stairs—and, if necessary, one at the bottom—will help a busy mother at this stage and prevent the risk of painful falls.

It is a pity to keep him pram-bound unnecessarily, but a light push-chair should be taken on walks for the under fours, to use

for the dull stretches, so that the child is ready to romp, and jump, and hop and skip when he gets to grassy places.

Physical Skills

Childhood is the time for the beginning of all kinds of athletic sports, developing skill, poise and confidence, as well as all the muscles (see p. 173). To practise throwing a ball into a large basket hung up for the purpose will give joy, but remember to encourage the child to use alternate hands, so that all chest muscles are brought into play. To learn to float and to swim can be begun quite early.

In the third year he will enjoy helping actively in the house. In the fourth year tree-climbing, hammering, and other semi-dangerous pastimes can be carried out under supervision.

Games, such as walking barefoot with books on the head, will help to develop a graceful healthy poise. Give him foot freedom when possible, but, when shoes are worn, see that they have flexible soles and fit snugly at the heel, but have lots of toe room. Beware of slippery floors and overcrowded rooms leading to bumps and falls. Balancing feats give joy and are very helpful.

Fatigue

Children tire very quickly and cannot hold one position for long. That is why it is unwise to tell a child to sit or stand still, and to be cross when he is not able to manage this. Instead give him a new interest.

When the family go afield for jaunts and picnics overfatigue should be guarded against. Children do not readily own up to it, partly from fear of being excluded from what's afoot, and partly because in their excitement they do not notice how eyes are straining, legs aching. It's up to parents to be on the watch for the symptoms, such as stumbling, shuffling, dropping things, crying easily, 'being awkward'. A ride on father's shoulder, or a break for refreshment if it can be arranged, is so much better than unsympathetic admonitions of 'I shall take you straight home this minute if I have any more nonsense!' or ineffectual and suggestive queries of 'Are you feeling tired, dear?'

XXV

TOILET TRAINING

IN EARLY INFANCY the emptying of the bladder is controlled by a reflex in the spinal cord. It is only as the nervous system develops that the brain gradually takes over responsibility in the matter. Messages from the bladder are not relayed to the highest level of the developing brain until baby is about nine months old. Many authorities advise postponing any so-called 'training' until about this time or even later. As, however, the body can adopt a pattern of behaviour before the mind takes over its conscious direction, and as repetition of an enjoyed situation is habit-forming, it would be wise to accustom baby to relieve himself in a certain posture, and at certain times, from fairly early days. After a feed the mother can hold him out comfortably, so that his back is supported by her chest, and he just touches the rim of the little chamber-pot held between her knees. This gives him a chance of bringing up wind as well as saving a napkin; it also gives the reflex action gentle stimulus.

If the child is found to be dry when brought in from a day nap, or when picked up for a feed, the little 'training' can be repeated, unless baby protests in any way. As the child grows the mother must be careful not to jump to attention *too* promptly in the matter! Children love to have mother 'at the end of a string', and if asking for the pot means that she comes running to them, they may use it for whim rather than for need.

Independence

As soon as the child can sit up alone his independence should be encouraged. His pot should be sufficiently large for comfort, and with a wide base to prevent toppling. To anchor it, it can be stood in an inverted three-legged stool; or father can make a box-seat to go over it, or there are special light frames on the market for the purpose. (Incidentally, to have a pot under the seat of the chair baby is using for meals is strongly discouraged.) Later, at about two and a half years, the child may like to use the lavatory, and special fitments, such as the Tot-seat, to give him comfort and security, can be obtained. If he shows signs of fear he should continue using his chamber until older, but if he can pull the plug himself he may enjoy doing so. A cord can be attached to the handle to help him.

Growth in control will be very, very slow. No set of muscles can be brought into good co-ordination in a hurry. Think of the months the child gives to kicking, crawling, standing and balancing before he attempts a single step alone. Remember the weeks of trial and error with spoon and mug before he feeds himself efficiently. Yet these skills are not as difficult for him to acquire as the art of learning to inhibit certain internal muscles at one time, and relax them at another.

At first the child is almost unaware of the need to relieve himself, but, round about fifteen months, he becomes conscious of warning signals, and also associates the chamber with the function. Urgency, however, is so great that often it is not until an 'accident' has occurred that he can tell his mother about it. Beware of considering this as 'naughtiness' on his part. It is just a stage in his development. In two or three months' time his recognition of the sensation of fullness will enable him to give a longer warning.

Bladder retention, that is the power of holding the urine, grows gradually. It will be about two hours at fifteen months. By two and a half to three years retention of some five hours is usually possible. At this time many children, if picked up at 10 or 11 at night, can keep dry till morning. Quietly observant, the mother should plan training times to fit in with the child's development, but should continue to take responsibility for accidents.

Primitive Interests

At about eighteen months children are specially interested in the products of their bodies and often want to examine, or even touch. The parents must beware of showing signs of disgust, snatching the child away, tapping the hands, and so on. An over-strict parent, who makes no allowance for primitive impulses, but can only 'love a clean boy' is doing serious harm to her child. He cannot bear to lose her favour and may inhibit his sense of touch and smell so drastically that he loses much creative ability. Later, instead of playing happily with mud pies or sand or clay, he will constantly ask to be made clean for he will be uneasy and with a sense of wrong-doing.

Children are very sensitive to mother's feelings. If they sense there is something unpleasing to her over their bodily processes they may wait until they feel safely covered with napkin or knicker, or go into a corner out of sight, or even hold back their stool altogether. All such emotional conflict can only hinder them in their struggle to get normal control over their bodily processes.

Because the organs of excretion and those connected with the sexual functions are closely connected, the child who develops a sense of guilt or uneasiness over the use of bowel or bladder may later on find himself ashamed and inhibited where the reproductive organs are concerned.

It is important then to keep training times short and happy, and to give the child as much freedom in regard to them as possible. Quiet pleasure should be shown at his success, but no tangible rewards offered. Equally, no crossness expressed over mistakes. Co-operation is the key-word, always remembering that a maturing bladder will train itself in due course, even without outside aid. Incidentally, it is wise to vary the routines when possible or the child may jib when travelling and visiting. To turn on a running tap may help him if he finds it difficult to relieve himself just when perhaps you are waiting to go out. Two special words which can be used to prevent embarrassment in company will usually be coined by the child himself.

The stools should be watched to be sure they do not become hard and thus lead to pain or straining. A correct diet should obviate this, together with sufficient fluid, but sometimes a little lubricant may be needed and if so this should be given by mouth. The use of enemas and suppositories are to be deprecated except in very special circumstances.

Giving up Napkins

As soon as the child starts walking in earnest the napkins should be converted into little pilches with a double centre-piece, which will be more comfortable, and less suggestive of baby ways. How soon to give them up at night must depend on the progress the child is making and also the time of year. With a highly strung child, in cold weather the warmth of the napkin around the pelvic area may be a preventive of wetting.

The majority of children are reasonably free from soiling accidents in the day-time at eighteen months, and from wetting ones by two to two and a half years. At night little girls are usually reliable by two and a half to three years, and little boys half a year later.

If after a period of freedom from accident the child reverts to bed-wetting or knicker-soiling, every part of his management should be considered, for treatment must depend on the root cause or causes. It can be taken for granted that every normal child wants to grow up and 'be big', so that nagging and urging should be avoided. To ensure that his sleep is as dreamless as possible, careful planning of the last meal, the last liquid, and the good-night mothering is necessary. His mattress should be reasonably firm and the child encouraged to sleep on his side, not on the back, and there must be moving air in the room.

The stools should be watched for worms or constipation. Warmth, especially of the feet, must be considered, but heavy, stuffy coverings avoided.

The bed must be kept sweet so that there is no stale suggestive odour. Sometimes the present of a pair of special pyjamas, or a new bed, gives the child that added self-respect that turns the tide for him.

Practice in self-management should be given from the age of three or so, and if there is no handy switch, a torch can be provided, while the chamber, a small light one, should be really handy.

In some cases to pick up about 9 p.m. and again just before the parents finally retire may help an individual child. If however he cannot easily fall asleep again this should be discontinued. Though tempting, it does not seem wise to allow him to pass water while he is asleep, or nearly so.

The unconscious takes over when conscious control is in abeyance so all suggestions given should be positive, peaceful and happy.

Listen when he tells you of his dreams, as these may give a clue to some underlying anxiety.

FOR FURTHER READING

Habit Training, from N.A.M.H., 39, Queen Anne Street, London, W.1, 1s. 4½d.

Training the Toddler, from 'The Woman's Pictorial', The Fleetway House, London, E.C.4, 2½d. by post.

XXVI

CHILDREN'S FEET

WITH LITTLE FEET wide apart so as to form the widest possible base, baby takes his first staggering steps, and then collapses with surprise. An exciting moment this, and what a lot has gone before to make it possible!

The vast majority of babies are born foot-perfect. In lands where it is the custom to go barefoot, they are almost sure to develop strong, firm, springy feet, which will carry them for miles, year after year, without the least discomfort. In our lands children are not so fortunate. For it is said that between 30 and 50 per cent of our adult population suffer from some form of foot defect—and that the chief cause of this is faulty foot care in early life.

At birth the 26 little bones comprising the feet are little more than gristle and their strengthening and hardening will be due to good nutrition and due exercise. Babies enjoy kicking, and the wise mother makes it easy for them to do so, arranging nappy-free times, being careful in tucking up the clothes not to compress the feet, and noting that overall-leggings do not constrict in any way.

As his back gets stronger, baby will bounce on his mother's knee with great content, she taking the weight of the body by supporting him under the arms. Daily she gives him chances to learn to 'swim', to roll, to creep, and to crawl, all of which bring the foot muscles and ligaments into play. At first a smooth warm surface is best for such actions, but, as baby gets stronger, it is good for him to crawl over uneven surfaces, to learn to clamber, and to experience various kinds of foot contact.

Going Barefoot

On carpets, and, in summer-time, on grass or sand, baby should go barefoot as frequently as possible, but the time is bound to come when the first shoe will be needed. No matter how soft it is, it still must be the right shape if it is not to slightly mould those

125

immature feet along wrong lines. So look closely at the child's foot, and note its outline—the curve of the line from heel to toe; the length of the big toe, the triangular shape of the forepart of the foot, and the width here compared to the width of the heel; also the depth of the foot, with its pad of fat. Note, too, any difference between the right foot and the left.

Choosing Shoes

Go to a good shoe-shop, and take baby with you to try on the shoes. The shoe you choose must take all these points into account. It should never have rounded toes, parallel sides, nor be shallow in depth.

When the time comes for the little one to walk abroad he will naturally need a sturdier type of shoe, but do see that it is flexible. Bend the sole where it meets the instep, and do not let the child wear it unless you can do this freely. Put your hand inside to see if it is soft and smooth all through. When it is on, note how it fits at the heel and instep, where it should be snug; and over the toes, where it should be roomy. The child should put his whole weight on the foot you are observing, for this will make it spread, just as it will do when he is trotting around in it. A gap between the big toe and the others should be possible.

A blocked toe-cap lifts the leather and gives the toes room to stretch and bend. A margin of a thumb's breadth from the end of the longest toe to the end of the shoe gives room for growth and ensures that the shoes will be wearable at any rate for 3 or 4 months without becoming too short. A correct inner border enables the foot to be laid down flat in the shoe with no inward thrust on the big toe. Outdoor shoes should be of the lace-up, indoor of the bar variety, to hold the shoe to the foot. Ankle straps allow it to slip about too much, so that it is not free to use all its energy to grip the floor.

The question of heels is a controversial point. In its natural position the foot takes the weight of the body on a level base. The grace and carriage of women who wear heal-less sandals, or go barefoot, and often carry weight on their heads, is very noteworthy. By putting a block under the heel, the foot rests on an inclined plane, and there must be some tendency for it to slide forward, while to keep the spine still in the upright position a certain tension unconsciously occurs. At least, see that the heels are as low and wide as possible all through childhood. Remember that the foot does not stop growing until about the age of fifteen, and does not reach full maturity until between eighteen and twenty-one.

A grip-like action is a great help when baby is learning to walk and it is easier for him to do so on a thick pile or on sand, or other material with a little give to it. It is not wise to attempt to teach him to walk, but friendly encouragement should be given when he shows signs of wishing to do so. If he has something to push along on wheels or domes of silence at times this frees him from concern with the question of balance, so that he can progress

Stage 1. Pulling himself up

127

with his little feet nearer together—useful for the developing arches.

Early Walking

A toddler throws his toes in a little when he first walks and this is helpful to the growing foot. It is if the toes are turned out that we must be concerned, for it means that the foot is tending to roll over, obstructing the arch, and hindering its full development. The final goal—for the toes to go straight forward, parallel to one another—will come in time if development is normal.

At first the whole bottom surface of the foot comes into contact with the ground. If this were to continue the blood-vessels and nerves which run under the middle sole would be affected by any shock or pressure to their detriment. A very high arch, however, is of no advantage, and such a foot often lacks flexibility.

Stage 2. Walking alone

Bow legs

Some mothers worry about the natural curve to the young toddler's leg, fearing that it is a sign of 'bow-legs'. This condition today, fortunately, is rare. The slight curve, which is still present from birth, is simple due to the pre-natal position, and with opportunities for stretching and kicking, the tibia, or leg bone, will in time grow quite straight. The mass of muscle which develops on the outer side of the leg give an impression of bandiness for a while, but this will be corrected with further development. Thus, as a rule, little need be done about so-called bow-legs or knock-knees unless, when the ankles are held together, there is as much as a 3-in. gap between the inner border of the knees. Consult your clinic or doctor if you are in any doubt.

Foot Exercises

A few special foot exercises, played as a game, can be instituted if any lack of muscle tone is discerned. Pulling on the toes, especially in the bath, with an accompaniment of 'This little pig went to market' is helpful in infancy. Later, pretending each foot to be a creepy-crawly caterpillar. Still later, picking up marbles, or folding a handkerchief with the toes, or lying on the back, throwing a ball and catching it with the feet, or jumping from a stool, landing 'like a cat', silently and with knees flexed. Given due opportunity, the foot becomes almost as dexterous as the hand, and keeps its original suppleness.

The National Baby Welfare Council, 31, Gloucester Place, W.1, have a useful illustrated leaflet—'Foot Exercises are Fun'—giving helpful suggestions. 4½d. by post.

If the child is heavy, a pedal-less tricycle, or the use of a low swing is often useful in encouraging him to use feet and legs without taking the body's weight at the same time.

Perspiration
The feet give off a good deal of perspiration, so socks should be washed daily, and shoes changed every time the child comes in from play. Two pairs should always be provided, to ensure thorough airing in between use. Wellingtons and plimsolls, useful for short periods and special purposes, should not be worn for long at a time. Leather, being porous, supple and hygienic, is the best foot covering; but, because of the high cost of repairs, as the child becomes more active, the leather sole may be reinforced with one of crepe or rubber.

There is naturally a temptation to hand shoes down through the family, but the correct moulding of the individual foot is so important that every effort should be made to avoid this. Again, no matter in how good condition shoes may be, they should be at once discarded if they are the least bit small. The same applies to socks. The feet are so soft that the child may not complain, but an unfortunate pressure is gradually diverting the foot—and particularly its main lever, the big toe—from its rightful alignment. Foot discomfort has such far-reaching effects on morale and nervous energy, as well as on physique, that no trouble or expense should be spared to safeguard the children's feet, even if it necessitates cutting down in other directions.

USEFUL ADDRESSES

Central Council for Health Education, Foot Health Educational Bureau, Tavistock House, Tavistock Square, London, W.C.1.
Foot Health Education Bureau, 121, Ebury Street, London, S.W.1.
Boot, Shoe and Allied Trades Research Association, Satra House, Kettering.

LEAFLETS

Foot Fitness for Mothers and Children, from National Baby Welfare Council, 31, Gloucester Place, London, W.1, 3*d.* plus postage.
Exercises for Knock Knees and Flat Feet, from 'The Woman's Pictorial', The Fleetway House, Farringdon St., London, E.C.4, 2½*d.*
Limb Massage and Exercises, from 'The Woman's Pictorial', The Fleetway House, Farringdon St., London, E.C.4, 2½*d.*

XXVII

LEARNING TO TALK

To BE ABLE to use his mother tongue freely is a task towards which a young baby bends a great deal of effort, and this is how it all begins. When he is about six weeks old the central nervous system first makes contact with his vocal cords, and he begins gradually to co-ordinate their movements with those of breathing. From then on the tongue, the lips and the soft palate are constantly put by baby into all sorts of experimental positions, with results in babblings, ah-ings, cooings, cryings—tones of all kinds. It is said that before a baby learns to pronounce his first words, at about eight months, he will have used literally hundreds of sounds—far more than he will need when he is actually talking. His first laugh —which, according to Barrie, was the origin of fairies—occurs at about four months.

Just as he enjoys sucking and swallowing, so baby enjoys producing these various noises, and, as he continually practises them, he gradually begins to shape them into sounds resembling words.

First Words

Da-da, ma-ma, are usually his earliest achievements. But proud mothers and fathers should realize that it is some time before a child can really attach a name to a person or object. And even then, for quite a while all nice men will be daddies, and all friendly women mummies!

As a rule the combining of two words to make a sort of sentence begins at about 18 months. 'All gone', 'Go bye-bye', 'Baby want', are some of the phrases coined at first. By the time a child is two he will be stringing really useful sentences together, and he will be quite capable of saying, 'I don't want to go to bed!'

Tests of good progress during this second year are not only the actual number of individual words a child knows (about 300–400 at two years is good); but also how he manages with pronouns, 'I', 'me' and 'you'; and whether he uses the past tense, and plurals, reasonably correctly.

It has been said that the two-year-old acquires words and that the three-year-old uses them, and certainly at about three there is a very marked development in his conversational powers. At this age the child not only enjoys talking, but he enjoys listening too.

The mother will now find that she can use words to distract a child's attention or to make a helpful suggestion. Prior to this age, talking largely 'went in one ear and out of the other'; but from three years it seems as if words hold a new magic to the child. Though he will still learn far more from dramatization than from reasoning, yet the latter now has its part to play in his management.

It will be years, however, before he uses words with anything like the same meaning that adults give to them. They have no 'associations' for him, for he has no idea of time, space and other matters. Experts tell us that we should not expect any child under ten years of age to be able to give a quite reliable, straightforward account of an incident. Before that time, imperfect observation, lack of discrimination and a vivid imagination will, between them, make his witness unreliable.

The 'Why?' stage, so exhausting to the average parent, begins about the third birthday and is at its peak between four and five. Busy and impatient elders too often fob the child off with some inadequate answer, or try to silence him, not realizing what a wonderful opportunity this is for sowing the seeds of all sorts of dynamic ideas, and encouraging an imaginative and knowledgeable attitude towards life. Of course, sometimes a child just asks questions to catch the adult's attention, or because he loves to hear the sound of his own voice, and to practise this thrilling new language, just as adults enjoy trying out their French or Italian. More often, however, he really wants to know; but if to the adult it doesn't in the least matter why the sky is blue, or why the clouds drop rain, or whatever it may be, then he loses the freshness and brightness of his interest in the marvels of the world around.

When the same question is repeated frequently in varying ways it means as a rule that there is a fundamental problem the child cannot express and which so far your answers have not solved for him. You can catch the underlying anxiety in questions such as

'What do people look like when they are dead?' or 'Can burglars see in the dark?'

Apparently silly questions may just mean that the child is in a silly mood, but they may point to his feeling of needing more attention than he is getting, or to some hidden anxiety.

Chattering

Parents should love to hear their children chattering—it is a sign of vivacity, of interest, and increasing intelligence. They must chatter 'far more than is good for them' if they are to get a really fluent hold of complex sentences, learn to put emotions and abstract thoughts into words, and how to express themselves in different situations. To check a child and impose silence on him; to refuse to listen to explanations; to snub him when he asks apparently meaningless questions; to be so discourteous as not to listen at all, or with only a quarter of an ear; all these things inevitably hinder a child from acquiring fluency of speech.

Of course there are times when silence is golden; but if tact is used the child is well able to understand and accept certain prohibitions, and while co-operating willingly, still to feel tongue-free and happy.

SPEECH DEFECTS

While there is an average pattern of speech development, variations are quite normal. Sometimes there is a family history of late or early speech. Sometimes a very contented child doesn't seem to feel the need to express himself verbally and is rather 'lazy' about trying.

Of two things we may be sure: that a normal child will understand hundreds of words before he is able to utter them; and that he will not be helped to talk by any sort of urging. Speech depends on the maturation of the nervous system; on listening to others talking; on good hearing; and on the need for making oneself understood.

The wise mother talks quietly, simply and cheerily to the child about all that happens in his little day. She tells him the names of things again and again, but does not ask him to repeat them. She keeps sentences very short. She sings him little repetitive rhymes and songs, and she does not rush to anticipate his needs, but lets him try to make himself understood.

In some cases talking is retarded or indistinct because the child does not hear the speech of those around him clearly. This may be because of deafness, tone deafness, or what is called high-frequency deafness. If the child always has difficulty with certain consonants, or if he doesn't hear what goes on behind his back, then expert advice must be sought.

Stuttering

A phase of stuttering, or stammering, worries many parents. Under four years of age it need not trouble them in the least. The hesitating repetition of a word, or the first syllable of a word, is quite normal, while the child is developing his vocabulary. Then, when he is about two and a half, he is at a stage where he has so much to say, and has not yet a great command of language, so that his words stumble out as it were. This tends to improve, but again, about a year later, becoming more critical of his own speech, and trying to express himself in grown-up fashion, he may waver and hesitate between some baby expression and one more grammatically correct, leading to stuttering.

Only harm is done if the parent checks the child, gets him to repeat the sentence, or in other ways draws his conscious attention to his difficulty. The same applies if the child uses a word wrongly, or uses a wrong word. To be highly amused—or shocked, or pained—is to underline and dramatize a phrase which would otherwise slip from memory.

Stammering

In an older child stammering is another matter and needs the attentions of an expert. We must not forget, however, that speech at any age can be easily disturbed by strong emotions. If your child finds it very hard to put his feeling into words, or to tell you about his activities, plans and thoughts, instead of direct questioning or reproaching, do realize that some emotional block may be occurring. Sometimes it is a feeling of inadequacy, sometimes suppressed hostility, or it may be just a fear of saying the wrong thing and being teased.

Learning to Talk

FOR FURTHER READING

The Stammering Child and How He Can be Helped, from National
Baby Welfare Council, 31, Gloucester Place, London, W.1, 3½d.
by post.
The Play Way in Speech Therapy, by Rodney Bennett. Evans Bros.,
3s. 6d.

XXVIII

CARE OF THE TEETH

BABY TEETH ARE not only a delightful ornament but highly efficient little tools. Baby will have two sets. The first, known as milk teeth, will number twenty; the second, the permanents, far larger and stronger, will ultimately number thirty-two. The order in which these usually come through is shown on the diagram opposite.

On a clean mouth, with good, well-spaced teeth, a clean blood-stream and a good digestion largely depend. You cannot take too much trouble to help baby grow strong teeth, and keep them in perfect trim.

Before Birth

The teeth are formed from the mother's blood. They begin to be laid down about the third month of pregnancy. By the time the apparently toothless baby is born he has his full set of twenty milk teeth hidden away ready to appear when they are needed. The permanent teeth, too, are already partially formed.

Thus, the foundations of strong, well-nourished teeth depend on the health of the mother—the foods she eats and her digestive processes generally. These foods can be summed up as milk, meat, fish, eggs, cheese, vegetables and salads, cod-liver oil, fruit juice and whole-grain bread and cereals. The mother-to-be must see that her own teeth are in perfect repair and avoid swallowing the poisons manufactured by an unhealthy mouth. To massage the gums regularly is especially helpful, squeezing between finger and thumb, or brushing lightly with a little salt and water. Dental sticks and floss are useful for cleaning between the teeth but great care must be taken not to irritate the gums in using these. For this reason, toothbrushes should not be too hard.

First Teeth

The eruption of the first tooth causes great family excitement.

Care of the Teeth

Usually baby will have been drooling, champing and showing signs of jaw discomfort for quite a time before that little white patch is seen. In some cases, however, the mother knows nothing about it till she hears the chink of enamel on cup or spoon.

From the first sign of eruption, or pushing through, until a tooth is fully grown, takes between 10 days and a month. The bigger teeth may take twice as long. Mothers often worry about the order in which the teeth appear, but really this has little if any significance, though it is usual for the two middle teeth in the lower jaw to come through first, and the two top middle ones to follow suit. They will be followed by two more in the lower jaw, so that the average baby has six to his credit by the first birthday.

Order in which the teeth are likely to appear

Second-year Teeth

After a while, two more teeth in the upper jaw come through, followed by the first four molars—teeth with rather large flat crowns—which arrive leaving spaces to be filled later by the four canines. The latter often come through at about eighteen months, just when the toddler is learning many important lessons, and therefore this is the time when emotional upsets should be dealt with in a mother's understanding way.

The last four—the second molars—come through at about two years and we do not expect bedwetting to cease until they are finally through. The arrival of the teeth is so spaced that there is an interval of two to eight weeks or more between each eruption, and in this way there is less strain on the system.

Exercise to the jaws should begin before the teeth are visible, to ensure proper development of the tooth sockets and sufficient expansion. Breast-feeding does, or should, provide this. The working of the little mouth against the breast massages the gums, and the energetic jaw-exercise involved widens the nasal passages and moulds the bones of the face beneficially. A well-toned breast does not give up its milk unless baby co-operates eagerly; to keep a pull on the nipple and encourage the child to be active at the breast is advisable. Sensible teething toys will help from 4 months.

Teething Troubles

The majority of babies have some discomfort when teething, particularly with the larger side teeth. It is a mistake, however, to attribute every upset, from six months to two years, to this cause!

Teething rings

If the gums look a little swollen, study baby at the breast and if it seems to hurt him to suckle, make frequent breaks, interspersing with a spoonful of smooth blackcurrant syrup, or puree, or a sip of cool water. If he is bottle-fed, enlarge holes in his teats, or try spoon-feeding. More fluid and less solids are needed, the giving of a little Dinneford's Fluid Magnesia has a cooling effect and helps if there is any delay in bowel action. Encourage a generous flow of saliva by tempting the appetite with colour, etc.; and instead of a hard rusk, see if baby will take a fairly soft crust from the top of the loaf. Many babies find it a help to have their gums gently rubbed, and special teething jellies for the purpose are on the market. Rubbing gently with a silver spoon seems to help, too, promoting more blood to the parts. A cool pillow-slip, if the cheeks are flushed, and cool moving air will prove soothing; while extra mothering should be given if baby is fretful.

Preventing Decay

Once teeth are cut, they must be both used and cleansed. Unused teeth are liable to decay. Soft, sticky, sugary foods are not good. Crisp, firm ones which won't 'go down' until they have been worked on with tongue and jaws and teeth are required. The teeth must have a chance to fulfil their function, and the change-over from suction to chewing and biting must be met by giving the child bones and unsweetened rusks and crusts on which to practise. It is better not to tip rusks with something sweet or baby will be inclined to suck on them rather than bite. Pulled bread, that is bread divided roughly into irregular shapes, and then crisped a golden brown in a slow oven, has advantages over the straight-sided rusk, in that it tends to widen the jaws.

Eskimos, who use their teeth from a very early age, not only for eating but in their work, have no word for 'toothache' in their language.

Avoid giving baby his food too hot for this is harmful to teeth and gums. Have his food as dry as possible, to discourage bolting. This will call out a rich supply of digestive juices, not only in the mouth, but also in the stomach and intestines. End each meal with something clean—a piece of apple whenever possible. Avoid soft clingy foods; if you must use them, clean the little teeth immediately afterwards. Never give a child milk and biscuits in bed.

Tooth cleaning

Races living on simple natural food under healthy conditions do not need a toothbrush. Alas, our complex, over-refined diet does not leave the mouth as clean and healthy as it should be. The toothbrush therefore becomes indispensable.

A toothbrush should fit the mouth and be fairly soft, a very small one being used at first. Keep it in a holder so that it dries in the air; and to rinse in salted water or to rub a little soap to a lather over the bristles and then rinse is good. Fine salt, alone, or combined with bicarbonate of soda (in the proportions of one part of bicarb. to two of salt), makes an economical dentifrice which is both alkaline and disinfectant, or plain water, or fluid magnesia can be used, and there are excellent tooth-pastes available. Baby must enjoy the rite but have no inducement to swallow the cleansing agent!

Since decay frequently begins in the sides of the teeth the brush must be used to remove all debris. Always brush up, away from the gums rather than across, or particles may get lodged between them.

Remember that a clean mouth is more important than a clean face. Few mothers would allow a child to go about with a sticky mouth or smudgy cheeks, but they are not so particular in allowing sticky, unbrushed teeth, just because they do not show!

THE PERMANENT TEETH

Round about two years of age the twenty teeth of the temporary set will be through, and on their care will depend the welfare of the permanent teeth, now steadily developing beneath them. It is a tragedy if any of those first little teeth must come out before they fall out of themselves, for the jaw will then tend to contract—when our aim must always be to make it expand, so that the thirty-two will find themselves no more crowded than the twenty. The closer they are together, the greater the chance of decay spreading and of the roots being correspondingly less strong and well nourished.

Sixth-year Molars

About the age of five the milk teeth should begin to separate, to make more room for their successors. The more exercise they have the better will this be done. The first of the permanents to erupt is known as the 'six-year molar' and it comes before any of the milk teeth have been shed. Placed just where the crushing power of the jaw is greatest, these four molars enable the child to chew harder foods and prevent the jaws coming too closely together. These are such important teeth that special care must be taken with tooth-brush drill when they appear, in order to minimize risk of decay.

As the front permanent incisors come through one or two at a time, from about seven years, the baby teeth are progressively shed. The full twenty will be replaced by about twelve years. Then four large molars will erupt between twelve and fourteen. The four 'wisdom' teeth come between the ages of seventeen and twenty-five, if at all.

The older child may feel teething stresses and need extra comfort at such times. Some children are distressed at the loss of teeth, so what is happening should be explained to them.

Dental Visits

With the right work to do, with the right food from which to draw building material, a child's teeth should be perfect, but a twice-yearly visit should be paid to a good dentist as soon as the twenty milk teeth are through. His expert eye will detect the earliest signs of tiny holes or weaknesses, and he can see whether the spacing is correct, or whether a little help is needed in straightening. Your child, too, can take a pride in keeping his teeth nice for such recurring inspections, and get an affection for the dentist's chair instead of a paralysing fear of it. The modern dentist is alive to the emotional problems involved in tooth attention, and sees that the early visits give the child that sense of friendly confidence which is so important to enable him to co-operate well.

Dummies

Readers of this book are not likely to be tempted to use 'comforters' for their babies, but it may be as well to list the possible bad effect of their frequent use.

The dummy tends to mould and raise the soft upper palate, narrowing the arch, and preventing the even eruption of the teeth, in well-developed jaws. It often leads to mouth-breathing and hence to a predisposition to adenoids. The damp rubber surface readily catches dust-laden particles. Constant sucking keeps up a continuous flow of saliva, not helpful to the digestion. Its use tends to cover up a child's real needs and give a false comfort. It often leads on to other comfort habits, so that baby is never happy without something in his mouth. Finally it spoils the look of baby's rosebud mouth!

FOR FURTHER READING

The Care of the Teeth, by G. Herbert Russell. J. Sherratt & Son, Altrincham, 2s.

XXIX

EYE DEVELOPMENT AND CARE

Colour

BABIES ARE ALL born with blue eyes simply because no pigment is present in the iris at first. If no pigment develops, the blue appearance—really due to a semi-transparent whitish layer, superimposed on a nearly black background layer—remains throughout life. In many cases a third layer of golden or brown pigment is developed. If this is thin or patchy, the child will have hazel or grey eyes; if it is thicker they will be dark brown or almost black.

Tears

The eyes of a newborn baby are immature so that he cannot see at all clearly. The twelve tiny muscles, by means of which the eyes can be moved right and left, and up and down, are as yet weak. The tear glands do not at first manufacture that warm, salty solution we call tears, which will continually bathe the eyes all through life, and which—in conjunction with the projecting brow, the eyelids and the lashes—guard the sensitive eye-balls from the greater number of everyday hazards.

The tear ducts, which drain the eyes, are not yet fully open. As they are not needed in the first weeks—until the tears start flowing—their development is often delayed. Should the eyes water a little at first there is not as a rule any cause for worry.

Eye Infections

Any eye discharge, should be reported to a doctor at once. Infections can occur externally, or internally through an infected, impoverished, or toxic blood-stream, and may need prompt attention. Any discharge should be able to come away freely, so as a rule a bandage or eye-shade is not advised. Should a fly or bit of dust get in the eye it can often be gently wiped away with a clean corner of a handkerchief dipped in boiled water; if it must be moistened with the tongue there is no need to be alarmed for the tears that will flow will speedily wash out any infection. A larger, sharper piece of grit, which might scratch the eye, is best dealt with by dropping in a little castor oil, or liquid paraffin, the eye being lightly bandaged to prevent movement. The child should then be taken to a doctor.

Bathing the Eyes

If it is necessary to bathe the eyes, always wash the hands well and use boiled water as the basis of any solution, such as weak Boracic lotion, or Optrex, which may be advised. Swabs of cotton-wool or lint can be dipped in this, then squeezed gently into the inner corner of the eye so that it runs through to the outer. The child should lie on a towel with head to one side until he is old enough to use an eye-bath. Pressure should not be applied over an affected area, but gentle pressure to the outer side—to help move the particle onwards and inwards—may be tried and blinking encouraged.

Styes usually mean the child is run-down and needs a medical overhaul. Extra vitamin B, in the form of yeast extracts, is often advised. The eye may need bathing in hot water, and, at night, the lids should be rubbed with a little Vaseline or Golden Eye Ointment, to prevent the lids sticking together.

Focusing

By about six months, eye and hand should be working together and baby should be able to focus the two eyes well together and not have any appearance of even an intermittent squint.

A squint means there is a weakness of one or more of the eye muscles and early attention is important, for a habit of looking in a certain way grows on a child. If he gets a double vision of an object he will tend to suppress one; this means that the weak eye will be used less and less until its power of vision may be lost entirely. To cover the good eye for a considerable period will give the weak eye the chance it needs to get stronger. Many children who squint are long-sighted, so glasses may be necessary to enable them to focus on near objects in an effortless way. Spectacles can be worn as early as 8 months, tying a light pair behind the head with tapes or elastic. Get your doctor to give you a recommendation to a good oculist, who can examine the eyes properly and determine the degree of the trouble and the best preventive treatment.

Some squints occur in later childhood, perhaps following an illness. Active steps must be taken to restore muscle tone and it is possible to get a child to co-operate in remedial exercises from about four years old. Patience and perseverence will be necessary and the eyes must be under expert observation for some time.

The growth of the eye goes on slowly until about the age of twenty-two and its shape is largely determined by heredity. If the eyeball is shorter than the so-called normal, farsightedness will be present. If, on the other hand, the eye-ball is longer than normal, then the child will develop shortsightedness, or myopia, making itself noticed particularly during school-days. The advice of a good eye specialist is needed if any difficulty in seeing clearly is experienced. Some forms of short sight (myopia) are progressive and strain must be avoided. An open-air life, not too close study of books, and a good diet will all help the eye to develop as normally as possible.

XXX

HABIT FORMING

'IN EVERY WORK the beginning is the most important part, especially in dealing with anything young and tender,' said Socrates—and any farmer, breeder, or gardener would confirm his view.

A little baby is innocent of all habits at birth but he very soon acquires a surprising number, which will prove either a help or a hindrance as he grows. Hence it is worth taking trouble to condition baby along wise lines right from the beginning.

Habits are formed partly through repetition and partly through enjoyment.—The one is not enough without the other. Or, to put it another way, partly through the pattern his mother unconsciously imposes as she sees to his needs, and partly to his own individual reaction to her handling.

The mother who fusses over her baby, nursing him in her arms or rocking him in his cot before he falls asleep, is conditioning him to expect stimulants before sleep can come. She who is haphazard, with no set plan to her day, is making it harder for her child to adjust happily to a simple routine, giving him a sense of security because he knows what to expect.

To try and impose a habit on a protesting baby, or to instil one for which he is not ready is, however, more than a waste of time. So the wise mother studies her baby and always respects his feelings, planning so that he gets enjoyment from what she decrees for him, and can thus make the desired habit fully 'his'.

The habit of obedience is rightly a very slow growth. If little children did as they were bid from the first it is probable that they would lose many an opportunity of finding out about life, of making experiments, and small moral choices of great value to them. 'Their's not to reason why' may be a good motto for a regiment of soldiers, but, with a developing personality, such short cuts are undesirable.

Obedience, however, should not be looked upon as an old-fashioned virtue, nor one which robs a child of initiative and individuality. As well ask a builder if he needs an architect's plans, or a gardener if a sapling needs a good stake, as ask a child to do without authority and firm guidance. The Fifth Commandment is the first with a promise attached!

The very lenient parent usually has a deficient sense of responsibility, adopting either the I-can't-be-bothered, or It-can't-happen-to-my-child attitude! The very stern parent usually has little understanding of the way a child's mind works and his true needs.

The wise parent builds obedience on an experience of happiness. That first little order, 'Come here, dear', should never be given if the child is to be scolded or deprived, but rather for something enjoyable, such as his fruit juice.

That second little order, 'Don't touch', should always be associated with the offer of an attractive alternative so that the child learns that mother's way is a pleasant one.

The habit of going to bed at a regular hour without a lot of fuss is one to foster, and consistency and regularity help tremendously. Also happy rituals to which a child looks forward—a tuck-me-up story, a confidential chat, perhaps a drink of fruit juice or a cup of Marmite, etc. The young child needs some ten minutes' warning so that he really has a chance to round off his play and is not brought back from the land of fantasy to reality too abruptly. The small choice is often the tactful way of getting a reluctant child to bath or bedroom. 'Who'd like a penny to go to the shop and buy a nice pair of pink pyjamas?' works well with one child—the penny, of course, being the invisible kind! 'Who's going to get upstairs first?' with another. The play spirit, carried out with zest and enjoyment, is not a sign of weakness—it is just a recognition of the fact that the under-eights have a vivid imagination—as useful as a carrot with a donkey!

Negativism

When the child discovers the power of the little word 'no' and enjoys experiment with it—running away when called, and showing other negative manifestations—the wise mother will refrain from joining battle. To introduce a similar situation from a surprise angle is usually all that is necessary, for a little child—not being able to think of two things at once—is highly divertable and suggestible.

Catch his attention and then try to make central the thing you want him to do. To take a very simple illustration: let us say you would like your child to start his meal with toast, he, shaking his head, demands bread. Forcing means a scene, unpleasantness, a dislike of the idea of toast in the future. Coaxing makes for stubbornness and flatters the child's will-to-power. To give in may not be wise. Your job is to make the idea of toast acceptable to the child, so that that of bread can recede to the outer margins of his mind; and the point be carried without conflict and thus a habit of obedience encouraged. Anything in fun, fact, or fantasy which enters your head can be used for the purpose—'Have you ever made toast on a long fork by a log-fire—shall we try one day?' 'I wonder where that toast would go in Hansel and Gretel's house?' 'I do believe that toast has two eyes but no nose!'

This principle of making central in a child's mind the thing we wish him to do has a double edge to it. It is often tempting to give instructions along negative lines. 'Now mind, I trust you not to go near the pond, or climb the fence, or swing on the gates' ferments suggestively in a child's mind until he finds himself paddling, climbing or swinging soon after his mother's back is turned.

But if, between two and a half and four years, in particular, the mother takes trouble to win a child's happy co-operation and get his will on to her side, his own law-abiding instinct will be so strengthened, and such a good relationship fostered, that obedience becomes more and more the normal reaction.

A Child's Feelings

Remember that *feelings* will last long after an incident is forgotten and that they tend to be cumulative—leading to one child developing a friendly, co-operative approach to life, and another a rebellious, sullen, or defiant one. Even the apparently docile, good child may, under this outer mask, be harbouring strong feelings of injustice, or fear—in the unconscious if not the conscious part of the personality. So never ride rough-shod over a child's feelings, nor seek to 'break his will', or go against the grain with him. And if you do so, do not think you have solved a problem and won a victory even if a habit is repressed for a time.

Habit Forming

Take the case of a small boy who takes an unpleasant delight in pulling feathers out of hens' tails and hearing their resultant squawks. Telling him it's naughty might well have no effect—words mean little to a child. Acting as policeman, and preventing him going to the hen-run, would work only while you were around. Punishing severely might make him pause out of fear of the consequences, but if, inside, he still *wants* to be destructive or aggressive, you haven't solved his problem. He'll pull the wings off flies, or squash snails, or take it out of a smaller child instead!

Obviously you've got to try and find out why he feels in this way. Possibly part of the responsibility is yours. He may have been made to feel inferior through sarcastic comments, or through being over-dominated and treated too strictly; he may feel your punishments a form of cruelty; he may be jealous of a brother or sister.

See what you can do to put things right, and try and arouse and foster a tender instinct to counteract the aggressive one. It can be his privileged job to prepare the hens' food and dole it out to them, to give them fresh water and straw, to collect their eggs, to shut them up for the night. Arouse compassionate instincts sufficiently strongly and, in time, hostile and destructive ones will fade away.

Self-control, that most important of all virtues, can be very gradually taught by example, and by a sequence of events—such as seeing that the child first washes hands, ties on bib, and says grace, before he starts to eat: is trained, as he gets older, to look and see if there's anything to pass to others and not just to grab and snatch for himself; not to demand snacks and sweets at odd hours, but to wait for mealtimes to satisfy his appetite, etc., etc.

As you daily help your child to establish habits that won't be tyrannical but liberating, won't be a clog but a help, do remember that weeds grow faster than flowers, and that the latter need more cultivating and care.

FOR FURTHER READING

Home Education (for the under-nine's), by Charlotte Mason, from the P.N.E.U., 171, Victoria Street, London, S.W.1, 8s. by post.
Thought Turning (as a factor in character training), by Helen Webb, M.B. from the P.N.E.U., 7d. by post.

XXXI

THE PREMATURE BABY

IT IS ALWAYS a pity if baby is born before the full nine months in the womb have passed. Towards the end of a pregnancy, therefore, particular care should be taken to avoid falls, or other accidents, over-fatigue, over-excitement, and poor diet. Should it seem that labour may be pending, the mother should go to bed at once, relaxing mentally and physically; and call her doctor, who may be able to avert matters.

The smaller the baby at birth, the less his chance of catching a strong hold on life, and the more skilful must be his nursing care. Given such care, however, in most cases the chances of survival are remarkably good; and—a cheering note—if baby gets through the first difficult month, and has few setbacks in the first year, he will become just as sturdy as if he had been born at full term. In fact, some research done in Sweden suggests that the 'prems' who survive are above the average, both in physical health and in mental and emotional stability. This may be related to all the special care lavished on them in the early months.

The aim of those in charge of the new little life will be to provide an environment which approximates to that of the womb. The premature needs above all humid warmth and oxygen. He has no power of maintaining nor regulating his own heat, no fat under the skin; to lose warmth is the biggest risk he faces. He must be handled as little as possible. Fluids and foods must be given very carefully in order not to risk vomiting or straining the immature digestive organs. Clothing must be very light in weight—gamgee tissue is often used at first.

Apart from his nurse and his parents, no visitors must be allowed anywhere near him. A good protective gauze mask (see p. 214) should be worn by whoever is tending him, for he has no resistance to infections.

Feeding

Breast milk is his best chance in life, so the mother should start expressing as soon as possible (see p. 20). There may be some delay until she has sufficient, and her doctor may arrange for supplies to be obtained through a milk bank run by a local hospital, or from a mother of a new baby who has a surplus. Any milk used must be boiled and diluted and given very carefully and slowly, in very small quantities—far better to give too little than too much. As a rule baby will be fed in the cradle, alternating the side on which he lies with each feed; he must never lie on his back. He may need as many as nine feeds in the 24 hours to begin with.

As he shows signs of becoming more active and of sucking better he can gradually be tried at the breast, and many babies as small as 4 lb. can be breast-fed in this way at least once a day, increasing to full breast-feeding at about 5 lb. in weight.

As baby will lack the iron normally laid down in the last month or two in the womb, he is generally given iron by mouth from about two months, and his need for vitamins is specially high.

Warmth

To conserve his heat, the room in which he sleeps should be between 70° and 80° F. day and night, testing by a wall thermometer hung near the cradle. The air should not get too dry and it may be wise at times to have a kettle boiling to prevent this. An open window will ensure a supply of oxygen, though this may be needed in more concentrated form in the early days.

The cradle must be kept equably warm day and night and to ensure this—unless a special incubator is being used—the sides of a small cradle should be lined with stout brown paper, and a blanket or piece of flannel be draped at the head. Three hot-water bottles will be needed, the one at the foot being the warmest. In rotation one must be filled every hour or so at first. Bottles should be placed outside the enveloping blanket, so that there is no possibility of their touching the child. His own temperature must be taken in the arm-pit at intervals, checking that it does not go below 97° or above 99°.

A mixture of cod-liver oil and olive oil is usually used for his 'bath' on his nurse's knees, and, even when he is strong enough to be tubbed, the less soap used the better as his skin is likely to be extra dry. To rub in a little lanoline or oil after the bath will help.

By the time the mother takes over many of these stringent precautions will no longer be necessary. They should be relaxed gradually, and as a rule by the time the baby is 6 or 7 lb. in weight he can be treated just as any normal child. He may be a little lethargic for some weeks and, if so, gentle massage from the wrist to the shoulder and the ankle to the thigh will help him, using an oiled hand; and all bodily movements should be gently stimulated.

All through the first year he will naturally be behind in passing his milestones, but there is nothing to worry about in this, providing he is making good progress. He will in all probability catch up to normal at eighteen months to two years, and, when he has done so, his prematurity can be safely forgotten.

XXXII

TWINS

ABOUT ONE EXPECTANT mother in every hundred produces twins, and about one in every thousand triplets. Twins may be either dissimilar—each being formed from a different ova; or they may be identical, growing from the one egg. In this case they will share one placenta and will be very alike, even having similar fingerprints. The rearing of twins is a fascinating task, but presents special problems, especially for the single-handed mother, who tends to feel overwhelmed at first.

A twin-birth should, if possible, be diagnosed in good time as extra preparations will be necessary, and extra care should be taken in the last weeks, remembering that twins usually arrive a fortnight before term.

Two cots are a necessity, for otherwise one baby is bound to rouse the other. If bed or pram must be temporarily shared the two should be laid top to tail, and not head to head, so that each has his own ration of unused air. A double pram will be useful for walks, but for morning sleeps in the garden each should have his own particular resting place.

Experience will soon teach the mother how best to plan the routine of the day so that each item may be accomplished in the shortest possible time. To save labour, not only for the sake of her own health, but also to ensure long unbroken intervals between feeds for her little ones, must be her aim. As a general rule, it will be found simplest to let the two babies share the same bath water, the one being dressed and put back in cot or playpen until the other has had his dip and necessary attention. With a second pair of hands such problems are, of course, greatly simplified.

Breast-Feeding
At first, each tiny twin must be brought separately to the mother so that he may have her undivided attention as he learns to suckle.

Later, comfortably supported in an upright position, both twins can be laid on a pillow, heads close, feet towards the hips, so that the two can be fed at once. This time-saving method can be followed when the mother is about, by sitting on a low chair without arms, or a stool against a sofa, and having the twins on pillows on her lap.

Should the supply at any time be deficient the aim should be to divide the available milk. The delicate mother, whose doctor warns her it would be a mistake to attempt to nourish both, should give

each alternate bottle-and breast-feeds. Baby A should have the breast at 6 a.m., 2 p.m. and 10 p.m. the first day, and at 10 a.m. and 6 p.m. the next. Meanwhile, Baby B has bottle-feeds at these times, having two breast-feeds the first day and three the next.

The more robust mother—especially if she has some help—will like to give each baby a breast and, after test-weighing, any complementary food necessary.

The third method, and perhaps the most generally satisfactory, is to fully satisfy Baby A at the breast, and put him down; then put Baby B to both breasts for a minute or two, finishing with the bottle. This gives the supply the best chance of drawing level with the demands—the fresh, hungry baby stimulating the glands to secrete further supplies; while, even if he only gets a very little, it acts as a digestive to the bottle-feed to follow.

Whichever method is followed, it is important to put each baby to alternate sides, so that both breasts get equal stimulation, and so that each baby has a similar chance.

Sharing Alike

This rule of share and share alike should be the aim all through childhood but it is easier in theory than in practice. One twin is almost bound to have a more winning personality than the other; one to be more placid, making less demands, and one to be stronger and more rebellious.

Allowing full scope for individuality, and studiously avoiding all comparisons, spoken or thought, the mother, as the presiding providence, must seek to be a model of justice and impartiality! What a thousand pities when little jealousies creep in to mar what should be one of the most beautiful and enduring affections in the world—that of twin for twin.

The sweetness of disposition one does often notice in wisely managed twins is possibly due to this opportunity of really sharing life right from the beginning with someone whose interests are so much the same—an experience denied the average child, whose playmate will always be a good stage ahead or behind him.

XXXIII
BABY'S LAUNDRY IN
THE NURSERY

To KEEP BABY sweet and clean means daily washing for many
months, so if some form of washing-machine can be provided it
will be a big help. A small hand-vacuum pump is a useful and inexpensive alternative.

If the water is hard it is well worth while finding some means to
soften it. This will save soap, be better for the hands, and keep the
garments soft and supple. A water softener can be installed, or a
softening agent can be added to the washing water. Calgon is one
such preparation. If soda is ever used it should be added ten
minutes before garments are washed, and the rinsing must be very
thorough.

Arrange for outdoor drying whenever possible. There are special
pulleys to go outside a window for flat users, and, with a little ingenuity a fairly large wash can be hung out in quite a small yard
or shed. Napkins dried out-of-doors need boiling less frequently
than those dried in the kitchen. In bad weather a drying cabinet
can be very useful. (Do not dry woollies near direct heat.) In frosty
weather the napkins and other cotton materials benefit from being
frozen, but silk and woollens go hard.

Airing must be thorough, and if garments can be kept in an
airing-cupboard between use, covered with a clean sheet, they
will not absorb fresh moisture from the surrounding atmosphere.
Always fold neatly when putting away, ready for use.

There are three possible washing agents—fine soap flakes; a
good castile or primrose soap, which can be turned into a jelly
(grate $\frac{1}{4}$ lb. soap, cover with 1 pint water, and heat gently until
dissolved); or one of the modern detergents. Avoid cheap soaps
and powders, which may contain harmful chemicals. Always rinse
very thoroughly.

Napkins should be put to soak immediately they are taken off, when they will be much easier to wash. Keep the soiled separate from the damped. If you cannot provide two pails with lids, make little containers from folded newspapers to receive the soiled napkin till you can attend to it. Then take to the toilet as soon as possible and flush well, using a special brush, before putting to soak. If the stools are green or loose, add a little disinfectant, such as Milton or Dettol to the soaking water, preferably warm.

Damped napkins are quickly washed in a little hot soapy lather. Rinse in two or three waters and hang out. To mangle will obviate the need for ironing and speed up drying. Soiled napkins should have the stained parts rubbed well, using a little good soap before washing. At least once a week napkins should be brought to the boil. Put in cold water with some cleansing agent, bring slowly to the boil and boil for ten minutes. Allow to cool, and rinse well.

Woollies and blankets should not be soaked before washing. To plunge into warm water before washing helps to prevent woollies matting. They should then be washed quickly in fairly warm soapy water, squeezing gently with the hands under the water, being careful not to twist the fibres, nor to allow the weight of the water to pull them out of shape. Rinse in two or three waters of as similar a temperature as possible and squeeze dry. Rolling in a dry towel is a good method of dealing with excess moisture without harming delicate fibres. Dry in a good current of air, keeping the article flat if possible, and in its natural shape. A hammock of coarse netting, or cord, attached to a rod at each end, which can be hung between posts, or even two chairs, is useful for the purpose. A clothes' airer on a pulley is very useful indoors.

Woollies, carefully washed, should not become discoloured or felted, but, should they do so, they can be improved by soaking for half an hour or so in tepid water, to which 10 vol. hydrogen peroxide (approximately $\frac{1}{2}$ pint to $\frac{1}{2}$ gallon) and a teaspoon of household ammonia have been added. Rinse thoroughly and dry in the open. A fairly bland, soapless detergent is also helpful in disentangling felted fibres. Try washing in one of these and gently pulling into shape.

Flannelette, if used, can be soaked in cold water for 10–30 minutes, put in warm suds and, if necessary, boiled. Never forget it is inflammable.

It is not a good plan to roll up coloured cottons when damp, for the dye may not be fixed. Rayon materials need quick drying, and these again should not be left rolled up damp. Nylon materials can be washed in hot suds, but only a cool iron must be used for them.

Stains are always a nursery problem. Cod-liver oil stains can be often avoided by using a large waterproof feeder, such as the Kleinert, or giving the oil when baby is undressed, or using a special spoon such as the Pop-it. If a drop is spilt, attend to it immediately with soap and water. If, however, it has penetrated the fabric, a grease solvent, such as carbon tetrachloride, should be applied to the part, which should be wetted first. If this fails, soak the stain 10 to 15 minutes in equal parts of hydrogen-peroxide (10 vols.) and water and then rinse well.

Many stains on cottons of a fast dye can be dealt with quite successfully by making a paste of a reliable detergent, such as Surf, and a little water. Leave on for half an hour and then rinse well. For fruit stains try moistening and rubbing in common salt. For grass stains soak in methylated spirits. For milky stains, sponge at once with warm water, otherwise a grease solvent will be needed. For scorch stains, apply a little glycerine, use borax when launder-ing, and dry in the sun.

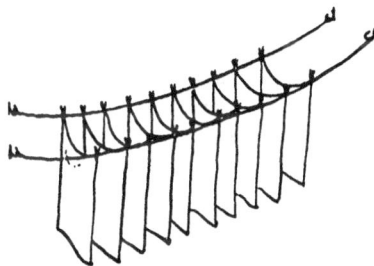

A space saving way of drying
napkins

XXXIV

PARENTS AND CHILDREN

FAMILY LIFE IS a delicate art. The interplay of the personalities of the mother, the father and the children, constantly changing and passing through new phases, requires much wise adjustment. The more satisfactory such relationships, the more charged with a feeling of warmth and affection, the more each individual will benefit. A lack of expressed love can do more harm to a child even than the withholding of food or of sunshine.

Fortunately most babies bring, as we say, their love with them. Nature wants her new nursling carefully protected during the early helpless years, and therefore she fills the mother's and father's hearts with the tenderest emotion towards their offspring. All the necessary labour and sacrifice involved in bringing up a child is sweetened and transfigured by the love-light through which that child is viewed, and by the happiness derived from the little ones response to their care.

In some cases, unfortunately, this happy relationship is early marred. It may be by lack of harmony and understanding; by mis-guided fears that expressed affection, fondling and cuddling may make a child soft, or spoil him in some way; by the transference of too much maternal feeling to the *new* baby; or by absence, ill-health and so on.

A child's capacity for making a happy relationship with others in later life, his belief in the fundamental goodness of people, his sense of inner security, his power to love and trust and co-operate with others, depend largely on home relationships which have either been warm, continuous, satisfying; or cold, broken and unhappy.

The Mother's Rôle

To begin with baby does not realize himself as a separate person —he is at one with his mother. But bit by bit, as he begins to distinguish the separateness of his personality, he is able to make good social adjustment just in so far as he has complete trust and faith in the one who cares for him, and longs to please her. If she fails him life fails him. If she rules through fear, and not through love, his whole personality will be maimed.

A mother's lap should grow in proportion to the size of her family. But growth of maternal feeling is not as simple as the unthinking or sentimental would have us believe. No two children are born to the same welcome. Family difficulties or ill-health may be occurring; the child's sex may be a disappointment; he may have an unfortunate resemblance to some disliked relation. The mother and father may be passing through a difficult stage in their own lives.

Which is more to be pitied, the child who is motherless, or the one who has an inner feeling of being rejected, and does not find in his mother's arms and heart his sure refuge?

The Father's Part

The importance of the father's relationship to the mother, as well as to the child, cannot be overestimated. Children are highly sensitive to atmosphere; they absorb it as a sponge absorbs moisture. If there is tension in the home, they become nervy and anxious. Later they may take sides, swinging dangerously from love to hate, acquiring a sense of guilt and fear in so doing. The idea of what a grown-up's life is like, what it means to be married, to be a parent, will be coloured by their observation of the life that is going on around them. According to their early experiences, they will later seek to escape from life, or be able to meet its challenges with confidence.

If parenthood is to have a welding and not a disintegrating affect on married life, the father's rôle should not be minimized. It must not be assumed that he is merely a bread-winner, and can have little part in the mysteries of babyhood. If at first the spark of parenthood seems lying somewhat dormant, the wise wife will gently fan it into flame, sharing with her husband many of the ministrations which baby's presence in the home involves, never for a moment letting him feel shut out or useless. Some husbands become jealous of their children when they see their wives so entirely wrapped up in their care—this is a very unfortunate foundation for a happy family circle.

It is only natural that mother comes first in baby's affection. It is from her soft breast that he feeds; in her warm arms that he most often finds comfort; her loving voice which reassures

when he wakes. In this initial stage, it is as the protector, the encourager, and supporter of mother—as chief actor in the family drama—that father must find his metier.

Sons and Daughters

Later, round about two years of age, the father should become an increasingly important figure to the children. A little son will seek to identify himself with his father, reproducing his stance, copying his speech, his very gestures, to the best of his ability. A little daughter will greatly love and admire her father, and seek to win his approbation. Round about the third year the small boy, very possessive of mother, may tend to feel himself a rival to father's claims on her, and thus become rather aggressive and resentful towards him. The small daughter may have emotional growing-pains, too, and feel jealous of mother's place in father's love.

Such phases should be met by loving understanding, not by any feeling of resentment on the part of either adult. Both little ones can be gently helped to accept with satisfaction their own special rôles in the family circle. It is a thousand pities if there is ever any suggestion that sons are more important, or daughters more attractive, to either parent. Or that mother is hurt when father is caressed, or father feels put out when no one but Mummy can content.

The parent-child relationship is never static; it is, or should be, changing almost continuously. A little child of two to five years cannot long be happy out of his mother's presence; everything he does is related to the need for her encouragement and approbation, for she is his goddess. Father, too is quite perfect. What 'my Daddy says' goes.

Growing Emancipation

But if the child is to develop to maturity he must increasingly grow away from such parent-dependence. After five the parent should not mean so agonizingly much to the child; he should have acquired some control over primitive feelings. In a year or two he will probably at times show dislike of demonstrative affection. He will tend to identify himself increasingly with his contemporaries, have friendships in his own age group, and experience interests in which the parents play little part. His teacher's influence, too, will be marked. All this weaning from home and mother, this gradual separating of pathways, is a normal healthy progress, steps on the ladder of growing up.

If the mother's love is possessive and she tries to shackle the child to her heart instead of setting him free to find his own place in the scheme of things, then she is doing him a serious disservice. The parents must learn to abdicate gracefully, to provide a steadying background without keeping the child on an apron-string.

Parents and Children

People as well as Parents

Wise parents constantly develop their own inner resources, culti-
vate friendships and interests among their contemporaries, and do
not lean their whole emotional weight on the children. They can
then give the gradual emancipation without a sense of friction
and personal loss. Parents should take a long-range view of life,
and realize that to bring up children, important as it is, is only one
of the tasks assigned them. The tendency to let the child fill the
whole canvas, as it were, and to occupy the whole centre of their
thoughts and affections should be kept in check, the mother especially cultivating herself as a person, as well as a parent, and having
outside interests whenever feasible.

ADOPTION

The question of adoption frequently crops up where a marriage is
childless. It may be a very happy solution, both for some little one
who might otherwise have no family background, and for adults
who are longing for a family. But it is a situation which needs very
careful consideration in advance. The best plan is to read some
of the excellent books and pamphlets written on the subject or to
get into touch with a reliable Adoption Society.

Adoptions are more usually and wisely made through a Registered
Adoption Society, or through the Children's Department of the
local Welfare Authority. But they can be made privately, with certain safeguards, though this plan is not usually a satisfactory one.

Legal Adoption Orders are given by special Courts, after a three
months' probationary period. No one under 21 can apply for an
Adoption Order. No baby under six weeks can be legally adopted.

The younger the baby, the greater chance of it becoming well
integrated into the family, but it is less easy to give an assessment of
probable development than it will be rather later. The early months
are, however, so important that the risk of some defect being missed
is well worth taking.

The health of the adopting parents is of even greater importance
than the health of the child, and a medical examination is impera-
tive to ensure that there are normal prospects of good health and
long life.

Parents and Children

FOR FURTHER READING

Troubles of Children and Parents, by Susan Isaacs. Methuen, 8s. 6d.

The Intelligent Parents' Manual, by Florence Powdermaker, M.D., and Louise Grimes. Heinemann, 10s. 6d. And in Penguin form.

The Young Child and His Parents, by Zoe Benjamin. University of London Press, Ltd., 6s.

Parents and Children, by Mrs. Nora Aris, M.A. Stanley Paul & Co., Limited, 8s. 6d.

You and Your Child. H.M. Stationery Office, Kingsway, W.C.2, 6d.

The Mental Aspects of Adoption. 10½d. by post from the National Association for Mental Health, 39, Queen Anne Street, W.1.

A Baby is Adopted, by Margaret Kornitzer, from the Church of England Children's Society, Old Town Hall, Kennington Road, S.E.11, 2s. 6d. plus postage.

What Should We Tell Our Adopted Child, 1d.

Standing Conference of Societies Registered for Adoption Report (1953), 5s.

Report of the Departmental Committee on the Adoption of Children. H.M. Stationery Office, 3s. (1954).

All three from Mr. A. Rampton, Gort Lodge, Petersham, Surrey.

XXXV

PUNISHMENT AND DISCIPLINE

THE SUBJECT OF punishment is one difficult to discuss quite dispassionately. We have all experienced it, and we have all reacted to it in various ways. Unhappy memories, unresolved resentments, may make one parent declare, 'I will never punish a child of mine!' May make another over-harsh and strict. Some folk are tough; some sentimental; some, afraid of their neighbour's opinion, punish to impress the woman-next-door rather than to benefit the child in question. Some, troubled with nerves, are so intolerant of childish noise, dirt and inevitable accidents that they relieve their feelings through scoldings and spankings.

What attitude should we seek to adopt in this matter? First of all, we must recognize that punishment is a Law of the Universe. You must reap what you sow. A child's training for schooldays, for life in the community, for spiritual growth, cannot be effected without a discipline which includes penalties for broken laws. Even the most 'modern' believer in free discipline, unless quite robot-like in personality, cannot fail to communicate a sense of disapproval for certain actions to a child—a real punishment to one who is sensitive.

Recognizing punishment as playing a vital part in training, we have then to ask ourselves what offences are punishable; how should we punish; and what effect should a punishment produce?

The fewer the punishments the better is good rule. It is more important to help a child to want to do what is right, than—through fear of retribution—to prevent him doing what is wrong. It is more important to keep a child's love, respect and confidence than it is to see that 'he gets what he deserves'.

Then, no punishment should be given unless it is certain that the child knew that what he did was wrong. And here it is so important to give enough time to discovering the child's point of view, for his actions should rarely be judged on their face value. Nursery literature is full of stories of children being punished for acts which the grown-ups considered crimes, but which, as far as motive was concerned, were really perfectly innocent or even commendable. A child has a keen sense of justice, and though it may be aggravating to a busy mother to have to listen to a badly expressed explanation in order to get at the truth, it is time well spent if the child's confidence in the fairness and understanding of the grown-up is enhanced.

Suppose a child throws a ball and breaks a window. Before punishing we want to know if it was an accident, due to poor coordination of muscles; a piece of restless mischief, due to lack of occupation—partly our responsibility; a defiant action, related to emotional unhappiness; or, sheer naughtiness. The feeling behind the halting, or glib, explanation will help you to decide; but, whichever way it is, the child should feel that it is the *action* with its unfortunate result that is disapproved of, not he himself, and that he hasn't lost any of your love or confidence.

Punishment, if needed, should be designed to help him to think and act more wisely another time, and to give him a chance of making some sort of restitution. Recrimination or scolding does not do this.

In general, before giving any punishment it might be well to ask: 'Do I want my child to suffer because he has made me suffer (by breaking my cherished possession, muddying my newly polished floor, shaming me in front of my critical relative, etc.) or do I genuinely feel that he is going to benefit from it?'

Bed should rarely be used as a punishment, because we do not want unhappy associations in regard to it; but arranging for some extra rest, or change of occupation, will prevent many a punishable act occurring. The over-tired, bored, or frustrated child is often unmanageably naughty. He won't be made better by punishing, only by removing the cause of his restlessness or aggression.

The Early Years
Naturally no punishment of any kind should be given in the first year. In the second, a firm 'No', or a removal from the scene, or of the offending article, is all that is necessary. Sometimes a light tap on the hand may impress and back up the 'No', but this should

165

not be necessary if the mother will take trouble really to catch her child's attention before she speaks, and if she helps him—by acting out the situation—to understand it. Or, if he wants to pull the cloth or throw his plate down, gives him opportunities of practising a similar kind of activity legitimately. In general a 'No' should always be followed with a pleasant alternative.

Physical Punishment

After the third birthday, when personality is established physical forms of punishment should, most experts agree, be taboo. The use of physical force and of pain is likely to set up emotional barriers, to teach a child to be rough with smaller children or animals, and to cause such distress or anger that, in his resentment or self-pity, the child quite forgets what he is being punished for. Spanking does not teach control through reason, but only through fear; and a child feels, often rightly, that he is being punished chiefly to relieve the parents' angry feelings.

Take as an example a nursery upset in which John in a fit of temper throws Mary's doll out of the window. A smack will tend to increase the angry impulse; a sentence of 'no jam for tea' will foster a sense of grievance against his sister and cloud the rest of the day. On the other hand, if, after he has cooled down a little, John is asked to put his favourite toy on a shelf until he has done what he can to restore the doll, and to comfort Mary, this will help him to enter imaginatively into the total situation and tend to improve his self-control in future.

Not to punish offends against a child's sense of the fitness of things. Children are great sticklers for law and order and like to feel that they will not be allowed to transgress without being pulled up firmly. The right punishment given in the right spirit gives the child a sense of relief; he feels he has expiated his guilt and the account can now be closed. And so it should be! Supposing you had broken your hostess's best coffee cup; merely saying you were sorry would not suffice; you would take endless trouble to replace it. But, having done so, you would not expect her to throw the incident in your face on future occasions!

Confessing

A child should be helped to confess a wrongdoing, not by asking him a direct question, which he cannot answer truthfully without a great 'loss of face', but by letting him feel you want to understand sympathetically why he acted in such and such a way. Confession —no matter of how bad an offence—should be met warmly and affectionately, so that the child may have his moral courage strengthened. Punishment should be as light as possible, but *some* punishment is essential. A child must not be taught to believe that an apology puts everything right—he must learn the difference between a skin-saving remorse and a true repentance, otherwise he may use 'saying sorry' glibly and insincerely.

Fitting the Crime
Punishments should as far as possible be brief, be immediate, and not be harsh. A mother should try to understand imaginatively something of what one will mean to a child. 'Well, you won't go to the party then!' may be a sentence of terrible magnitude to a child—quite out of proportion to the peccadillo which prompted it.

A punishment, however, should not be so light that the child hardly feels it! Above all, it should be felt by him to be strictly fair and reasonable. To ensure this sometimes it is wise to allow the child himself to choose it. Finally, it should be given with the minimum of fuss—because some children crave limelight so much that they repeat offences in order to obtain it.

Excessive lenience on the part of parents is a definite disservice to the child for which he will not thank them in later life. The child allowed to get away with all sorts of indefensible acts is not having a good moral conscience built up, to steady and stabilize him in times of temptation; not being prepared for responsible citizenship.

Perhaps we may sum up by likening the spirit of a child to an elemental force, such as water. Left to itself it will spread this way and that and do much damage. Canalized, harnessed and disciplined, it will be a wonderful power for good.

Punish then, not to burden your child with fear and guilt, not to discourage or shame him, not to relieve your feelings, but to help him to grow strong and straight, more clearly discerning between good and evil, and choosing the former to the best of his ability.

FOR FURTHER READING

Modern Child Psychology, by Agatha H. Bowley. Hutchinson's, 7s. 6d.

Bringing Up Children, by Kathleen Baron. English Universities Press, Ltd., 6s.

Child Management, from 'The Woman's Pictorial', The Fleetway House, London, E.C.4, $2\frac{1}{2}d$. by post.

XXXVI

PLAY AND TOYS

To SAY OF a child 'he is only playing' is to miss the wonderful value of the delightful and deep-rooted instinct with which, as with all young things of any intelligence, he is endowed. It is through play that he learns, finds his feet, gets co-ordination over muscles, acquires balance, poise and purpose. Play is a serious matter to a child and to treat it as something which can be interrupted or stopped at whim, and generally of little importance, is to make a grave mistake.

Room to Play

Even in the smallest home some space for play should be arranged, pushing back or rearranging furniture to make this possible, and providing each child with some box or cupboard to hold his treasures. If it is possible to set apart a corner where play material can be left undisturbed overnight it is splendid. A yard, copse, or field where outdoor games can be carried on free from restrictions, makes a fine playroom for the older child.

Toys

A child's play needs are constantly changing, so toys should be chosen with the idea of helping him to make the best of the stage of development he has reached. Those for which he is not yet ready baffle and dishearten; those he has outgrown, bore and encourage a destructive tendency. Too many toys can be harmful—the child flits from one to another, missing the chance of developing ingenuity and of learning to concentrate. Toys which are quite complete are of less use to a child than those on which he can exercise his creative or constructive faculties.

Because play is a child's apprenticeship to life all his toys should be simple and strong. It would be difficult for an apprentice to become skilful if given tools which soon bent, buckled, or snapped under use. Sound workmanship, smooth finish, clear harmonious colours, durable materials, give a child a training in good taste and functional fitness of real value. Crude colours, flimsy, inefficient structures lay no such foundation. Because they won't work they sap a child's confidence in his powers of achievement; because they break so easily he becomes careless and indifferent.

The First Year

As soon as baby starts reaching out after objects he needs his first simple toys. Teething-pegs and beads, musical rattles, balls of soft wool, animals with a squeak, something to watch waving in the breeze—all these will intrigue and stimulate his activities. Safe surfaces, suitable for sucking and champing, are essential, with nothing detachable or fluffy which could be swallowed, nothing heavy; no sharp edges.

Once the crawling stage is reached, the interest of throwing and pursuit is aroused. Rubber dolls or ducks are good for this, soft, safe and scrubbable. When the child is sitting up strongly with a good balance, the instinct to explore and rummage will come to the fore. The ex-baby will delight in cupboards, or boxes with lids, to open and shut, to solemnly empty and fill. Treasures to strew around and amass can be simple household ones—patty pans, odd lids, empty cotton-reels, spools, well-washed containers, fir cones, and so on. Variety of texture, shape, weight, colour, will all help to train the senses and give endless delight.

The Second Year

As he gets on his feet and learns to walk, toys which encourage movement are needed—something on wheels, firmly based, to push or pull along is always popular.

Very simple constructive play begins round about fifteen months. Light bricks to poise one on another, pegs to push into holes, shapes to put through slots, beakers to fit into one another nest-wise, a hammering toy—anything that he can manipulate very easily, poking, pulling and taking apart will appeal. The very simple picture-tray, the forerunner of later jigsaw, now gives great pleasure. The ball for this age should be large and light and preferably of sorbo material.

Play and Toys

At eighteen months the toddler wants increasingly to copy the grown-ups, so miniature replicas of any garment or gadget, worn or used by Daddy or Mummy, will give the greatest satisfaction.

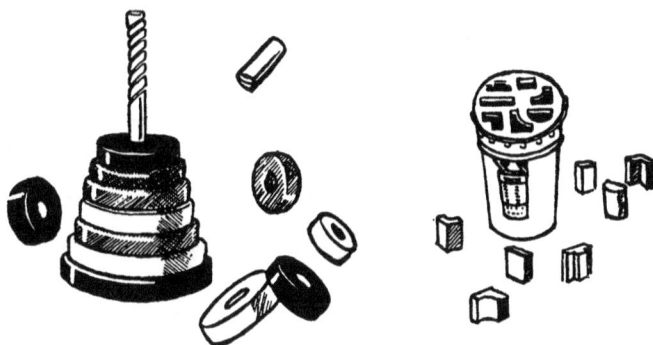

Later, as his imagination grows and his circle widens, the equipment used by other folk in their jobs attracts—the postman's hat and bag, the conductor's ticket-punching outfit, the milkman's cart and bottles.

Educative Playing

Round about the age of three-plus the choice of material widens considerably. Bricks can be provided in great variety, with trucks to wheel them around; bright poster paints and large brushes, or crayons, together with blackboard paper, or a scribbling wall, will be needed. Plasticine or clay, a sandpit, blunt scissors, garden tools, a tent or other apparatus for making a 'home'; a pastry board and tea-set; toys which screw together to build into working models; mosaics and jigsaws to exercise brain and eye. Many semi-educational pieces of apparatus, such as simple weaving, or embroidery on pricked cards, will often give more enjoyment than the toy pure and simple from now on.

Learning by Doing

There seem to be special times in a child's development when he becomes ready for a particular activity. If given the right exercise-material he will occupy himself indefinitely and feel at peace with himself and his world. If you are not always able to afford special apparatus, do let him play with your 'toys' as far as you can, and forbear to use that little word 'naughty' when some of his efforts—to clear away the tea-things, to wash the floor, or sweep up the crumbs, come to a disastrous end. He can only learn by doing. Refuse his early offers of help, and, later on, you may find that he appears apathetic and lazy and with no desire to take any share in running the home.

Toys to Love
A growing family of dolls, or soft animals, is important to a child from an early age. He projects his personality on to them and endows them with life and character. One may be a comforter, one

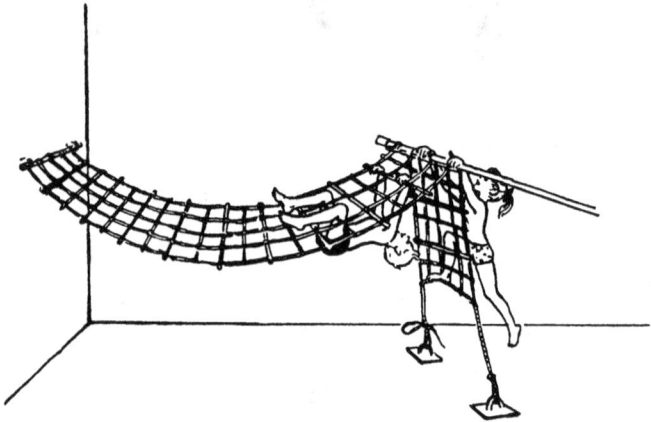

A commando net

a playfellow, another a whipping boy. Children pick their own favourite buddy with some special instinct which has nothing to do with the beauty of the beloved. Never belittle such strong attachments, and if a shabby object falls to pieces, renovate skilfully and do not treat it as worn out.

Miniature farms, stations and shops appeal strongly to a child just discovering the world around him. This is partly because everything is so more-than-life-sized in his eyes, and to be able to study the whole tree, or the telephone kiosk and make them move here and there, according to his fantasies, gives him enormous satisfaction, and compensates to some extent for the fact that he himself is so continuously 'under authority' and moved around by others.

The 'feelings' of toys should be respected as later those of pets. Teddy must not be left sprawling in a dusty corner, dolls must be tucked up for the night, books be put away right side up with no dog-eared pages, bricks and jigsaws returned neatly to their respective places. Don't make this a disciplinary matter, when it may become a nightly battle! Encourage the child to adopt the rôle of

A simple chute

director of proceedings, and lend him your cheerful aid, just as you wish him to help you when you need it. Interest and competence will increase until the habit of tidying up becomes second nature.

Gymnastics

Toys to help physical growth, climbing, balancing, swinging, are especially valuable where there is not much space, and where a child does not go to a nursery school or play-centre. Jungle gymns, chutes, etc., can be bought or made, but less expensive substitutes can be rigged up with a little thought and care. A box firmly fixed, with a well-planed, movable board to put against it will act as see-saw or chute; a stretcher-bed inclined against a play-pen; a firmly built rail, or light frame supporting horizontal rods, to hang from; a commando net to climb about on; a short ladder fastened securely to a wall at about three feet in height—these are suggestions.

Do not spoil the naturally adventurous spirit of a fearless child by a deadening, safety-first policy. Children have a good instinct for what they can or cannot tackle and a native caution, if they are not badgered with too many adult warnings. A few tumbles are a small price to pay for lessons in courage and poise which a little one, given freedom to experiment, can learn.

Wheeled toys give endless joy. A pedal-less tricycle gives good exercise to small feet and ankles. The larger tricycle should be fitted with reliable brakes if it is to be used outside the garden. Before he is allowed a fairy cycle the child's road sense should be trained. A kite to fly is an old favourite that is beloved of each generation in turn.

Playing shop is a useful way of helping a child to acquire some idea of the difference in value of various coins. At first he is quite mystified on the subject of change and the difference between the farthing or threepenny bit, the florin or halfpenny. Toy money can be a real help here.

There is, however, no way of really learning the value of money except by having control of some and actually spending it. Educating in managing money is something too often neglected, and a well-known banker has declared that most folk are 'economic illiterates'. Every child from five years should have regular pocket money which is really his own.

Pocket money is best given in the form of 'change', so that the child if he wishes can plan to save some, use some for presents, to 'put something in the collection', to spend something on his passing whim, or to put by something towards a larger purchase. Of course he won't be wise in these matters all at once! In fact, he can only learn by making mistakes. Until he has lost some money he won't appreciate the value of a strong purse, or a fixed money-box. Until he has spent all on a Saturday, forgetting Mother's birthday on

Play and Toys

Thursday, he won't get a habit of thinking ahead. He has to gradually discover what money will or will not do, and the ratio between his wants and the economics of his situation. It's harder for the modern child—and his parents—when prices are both high and fluctuating.

To be too generous or too skimpy; to allow the child much more or much less than his contemporaries, is never wise. But he should feel his parents are in sympathy with his projects and ready to help him to earn a little extra when necessary. When any money is given him he should feel it really is his and it should not be banked for him against his express wish. In fact, he should be educated in the use of money gradually and allowed to develop resource, initiative, carefulness and generosity in regard to it.

FOR FURTHER READING

Playtime in the First Five Years, by Hilary Page. Allen & Unwin, 12s. 6d.

Making Nursery Toys, by Nancy Catford. Frederick Muller, 5s.

Days Without Toys. Nursery School Association, 1, Park Crescent, Portland Place, London, W.1., 9d.

Educational Value of the Nursery School. Nursery School Association, 1s.

Play with a Purpose. H.M. Stationery Office, Kingsway, London, W.C., 1s.

Play, Toys and Discipline, by Beatrix Tudor-Hart. Routledge & Kegan Paul, 10s. 6d.

XXXVII

THE FACTS OF LIFE

EVERY NORMAL CHILD is endowed with a healthy thirst for know-ledge, a big bump of curiosity, and a keen desire to try and piece together the facts he acquires, so as to get some understanding of this puzzling universe. He learns some facts of life every day, but whether he learns them helpfully or not depends on his natural teachers—his parents.

Before self-consciousness comes in to erect barriers; before the mind is full of secret reserves; they have a wonderful chance to plant seed-thoughts of the loveliest kind, which sprouting in later life, will safeguard the individual from a too-materialistic—and hence pessimistic—outlook on life, its purpose, and goal.

It isn't difficult, even with a town child, to open his eyes to some-thing of the wonder of the whole cycle of life and death going on around him. He has first to distinguish between the things which are alive and those, like sticks and stones, which are not. Then he has to discover that everything that is living can reproduce itself, but that it takes two to do it. There are lots of helpful books on the life stories of flowers, birds and insects, through which these truths can be happily brought home. The child taught to look and listen and take an interest in all that goes on around him is being started on a thrilling life interest; while Nature's parables will give him a basic philosophy of very great value.

Death

The discovery of death will come early. The flowers he picks wilt; even those in water soon die. Other flowers reappear year after year, for there is life in the hidden bulb. So he learns that death may be of two kinds—one a sleep, and one a final end. How to deal with the possible loss of the child's loved ones will be considered later on in the chapter.

The child lucky enough to keep rabbits, or guinea-pigs; able to

The Facts of Life

bring in the hens' eggs, and watch chicks hatching out; to collect frogs' spawn and study its transformation viâ tadpoles into full-grown frogs; to watch bees laden with pollen flying from flower to flower—will find it easier to learn about the reproduction of life than one who learns of these things only at second-hand, if at all.

The Story of Birth

That important question, 'How was I born, Mummy?' usually occurs round about three years of age. It is not then the time to talk about bees, or flowers, or even mother cats and kittens. The child's straight question should get a straight answer. Simply, lovingly, and with some gusto, the happy story of how he began as the tiniest little egg, in the warmest, softest and safest of all possible places, should be told him. How he grew and grew, and got bigger and bigger, until the great day came when he was born, and lay in the lovely little cradle that had been got ready for him. The story can and should be embroidered with all sorts of happy detail, always stressing the joy of it all, and the welcome given to the child. Daddy's part in planting the seed can and should be mentioned, but to the child at first it has little significance. The two *dramatis personae* are himself and his mother.

Never think that once you have told your child he 'knows'. The story will need re-telling many times as his power of absorbing a wider range of ideas grows, and as, having chewed it over in his mind, and brought his vivid imagination to bear on it, this or that query arises.

Questions

The way the child's first questions are answered matters very much. Not because of the facts, which he may easily forget, but because of a fundamental emotional feeling he receives. If he feels that mother is embarrassed, then he will feel shy too. If he feels she is putting him off, then he is likely to take his questions elsewhere. The child who never asks about the story of his birth has, you may be sure, built up an emotional barrier, or has pushed the desire to know right out of his conscious mind. The mother should try to be relaxed and happy herself, to avoid being dogmatic, or telling him too much at a time. In fact, not to seek to be more explicit or earnest than she would be if she were being asked how a leaf grew on a tree. And yet if, without moralizing or being over-sentimental,

177

something of the mystery of life, and the reverence due to its great value can be conveyed to the child, it will be very worth while. Treated in this way, the little one will be ready to accept the story of a coming baby as a family secret. Children have an intuitive understanding of such things, and are ready to take their cue from their parents.

The child who blurts out questions at an inconvenient moment is often out to shock, and it's generally a sign that he has some resentment in his little mind that should be resolved for him.

The child who asks the same question over and over again is rarely seeking for facts, but for reassurance in regard to some hidden worry. The ultimate problem that besets his mind is the security of his relations with his Mother. 'Do you love Daddy, or the elder brothers and sisters—there before me—more than me?' 'Can I disappear again, or will you disappear?' Thoughts of this character give an emotional colouring to some surface question, which seems trivial to the adult, but seriously worries the child.

The Child's Body

For the first eight or nine years, information along fairly general lines is all that is needed as a rule, but preparation for discussing the part the Daddy plays must go on quietly, and a clear idea of the difference between the two sexes be established.

Little ones should see each other undressed. Up to the age of six or so they should bath together and have time to examine their own and other children's bodies freely. Primitive impulses and curiosities must find some satisfaction before they can be healthily sublimated. The child who in later life is a peeping Tom has usually been taught a false modesty in early days.

To teach the right names of every part of the body will be a safeguard against a furtive approach to these matters at a later stage, as well as making it easier to answer questions as they crop up. It is important to be sure that neither boy nor girl imagines one kind of body to be better or more complete than another and lots of children do have fantasies of this kind. Little boys often develop fears that they may be mutilated by an angry parent and turn into little girls; while their sisters easily develop an inferiority complex about themselves. Encourage each child to anticipate with pleasure the goal that lies ahead. Girls are made one way so that they can grow up to be mothers, and boys another in order that they may become fathers. Children are very suggestible, and deep contentment with their lot—or a restless wish for change—lies largely in the hands of the parents. If either parent has been disappointed in the sex of the child, an unfortunate sense of dissatisfaction may be passed on.

If a little girl constantly tries to ape her brother and wants to have her hair short and wear trousers; or if a little lad is too bound to his mother's side and wants to play only with girls and share their interests, parents should be on the alert to help them to make a happier identification—the boy with his father, the girl with her mother.

The over-possessive, over-dominating, neglectful, or rejecting type of parent, makes it tremendously hard for a child to achieve full masculinity or full femininity, able to marry happily and found stable families themselves.

Father's Part

Let us hope pleasant ideas are associated with the word 'Father' all along. Sad if when father enters the door, fun and freedom fly out of the window. If he is used as a sort of judge or policeman, and if the children's main aim is to make themselves scarce when he is about. We must remember that the roots of religious experience lie in the relation of the child, first to his mother, and then to his father. The child who has never adored these earthly guardians, will find it hard ever to worship his Heavenly Father.

In the fish, bird and animal worlds the rôle of the father can be shown to be protective as well as heroic. The father bird fetching worms for his hungry offspring; the stickleback male actually building the nest; the father wolf standing guard over the cave where mother wolf tends her cubs, and so on. It is far more important to get across to the children the idea of the love existing between the partners and their care for their young, than to burden them with the exact method of mating.

This side of the picture, especially where human mating is concerned, dwelt on too soon, may cause some sense of anxiety or shock. Knowledge given prematurely can be harmful, like prising open a bud before its time. On the other hand, knowledge withheld, or worse still, distorted, can harm in another way. It is good for the

179

child to have a clear idea of the story of human birth before puberty —before he himself is emotionally involved. An understanding and fundamentally clean background of facts safeguards the schoolboy or girl from smutty talk and innuendos from less well-instructed companions.

Masturbation

Here perhaps the question of masturbation might be considered. This starts in most children quite naturally as they handle the various parts of the body, and find a pleasure in so doing. It can and should be outgrown and forgotten as the child grows and leads a full active life, though it will probably recur at adolescence.

A watch should be kept that the sensitive parts of the body are not over-stimulated by a constant pull on the fork from tight garments; by too many games of the Ride-a-Cock-Horse variety; by local irritations, due to lack of cleanliness, or the presence of worms, etc.

Beware of leaving the child bored and unoccupied for long stretches of time, and always let him take a favourite toy to bed.

Checking by slapping, or scolding, should be avoided, for that would mean the child would be all the more likely to practise it— only round the corner. If a sense of guilt or emotional disturbance is associated with a situation it is harder to forget and to leave behind.

In general the habit is a comforting one, practised when the child is lonely, worried or tense, and to ease such situations for him is the most helpful plan. Be sure that he has lots of material to mould and shape and handle in the way of putty, dough, or clay, sand or earth. Let him practise that sensitive touch-perception of his on different textures and materials: the very soft, such as fur, velvet or satin; the smooth, such as linen or polished wood; the rough such as hessian or emery paper, and so on. Never worry about the habit, nor fear there is something wrong and precocious about your child. Just seek to provide stronger and more delightful interests and build up self-confidence, self-respect.

What about the so-called sex-play in which many young children find delight? Doctors and nurses, births, weddings, funerals, operations, and so on? A friendly eye can be kept on these games to introduce a new turn to the play if it is getting rather intense, but, in general, no interference will be necessary with a normal group of healthy youngsters. They must play at life if they are to attempt to understand it.

Meeting Death

The last 'fact of life' to consider is the question of death. No attempt must be made to hide this natural end of all things from a little child, and he can be helped to see how impossibly full the world would become without it; to appreciate how there comes a time when folk are tired and glad to lay their worn bodies to rest. But this, like taking off clothes to go to sleep, does not mean the end. The little philosopher can be asked to say which part of him is the 'I'. Is he still 'himself' when asleep? Or if he were to lose an eye, or a foot, or a hand? He can be shown how we do not forget folk when we cannot see them and that love is not dependent on bodily sight.

The story of the grub turned into a beautiful butterfly; or the dragon-fly who climbs from the murky pond to spread his glowing wings in the upper air will help, too. Happy the parents who have a strong religious faith and can teach a child about the Father's House with its many Mansions, and about the Tender Shepherd who has gone before to prepare a place there for each one.

The child who has the sure and certain hope of the Resurrection will find it less hard to bear an earthly sorrow, and there will be more channels of comfort open to him. That sorrow, however, should not be hidden from him. The mother who keeps a stiff upper lip over a personal loss in order not to distress her child may do him a disservice. To him it will seem that she is callous, and does not really care. Any emotion can be enriching; any dammed back at the source impoverishing. Time is, however, a great healer and little children should never be expected to show a grief they do not feel spontaneously, nor should their days be clouded by any conventional forms of mourning.

Naturally it is never right to deceive a child and tell him a tale about Granny having gone on a visit and being back soon, or anything of this kind. As far as possible all mysteries should be avoided and the child take his share in each family situation. In the unfortunate case of the loss of a father or mother, every effort should be made to bring some substitute parent into a child's life.

To sum up, the best way of teaching the facts of life is for the parents to live well adjusted and God-fearing, happy lives, from which the children can derive a good pattern. Always bearing in mind that the children are not 'their's', but are, as it were, in trust. The goal—not that they become devoted daughters and wonderful sons, but independent and upright citizens, founders of happy homes in their turn.

FOR FURTHER READING

How a Baby is Born, by K. de Schweinitz. Routledge & Kegan Paul, 4s.

Wonder of Life, by M. I. Levine and J. H. Seligmann. Routledge & Kegan Paul, 4s. 6d.

Being Born, by F. Bruce Strain. Arthur Barrow, 50, Carter Lane, London, E.C.4, 8s. 6d.

Preparing the Family for the New Arrival. Central Council for Health Education, 2d.

What Shall I Tell My Child? Central Council for Health Education, 1s. 3d.

Telling Your Children, by Dr. Enid Smith. The Alliance, 3d.

Growing and Growing Up (Girls), by Tucker and Pout. The Alliance, 1s.

Growing and Growing Up (Boys), by Tucker and Pout. The Alliance, 1s.

Children's Questions. S.P.C.K., 9, Northumberland Avenue, London, W.C.2, 1s.

The Story of a New Life. S.P.C.K., 4d.

Where Did I Come From?, by Hugh C. Warner. Student Christian Movement, 6d.

How a Family Begins, by Hugh C. Warner. S. C. M., 9d.

The Start of a Family, by Hugh C. Warner. S. C. M., 9d.

Simple Advice to Those About to Marry. Miss Pemberton, St. Cedds, Ingatestone, Essex, 2s.

Note: Postage extra in all cases.

ADDRESSES WHERE LITERATURE IS OBTAINABLE

The Marriage Guidance Council, 78, Duke St., London, W.1.

Central Council for Health Education, Tavistock House, Tavistock Square, London, W.C.1.

The Facts of Life

The Student Christian Movement Press Limited, 58, Bloomsbury Street, London, W.C.1.

The Alliance, 238, Edgware Road, London, W.2.

The Scottish Alliance, 8, Hope Street, Edinburgh.

XXXVIII

BROTHERS AND SISTERS

IF BROTHER AND SISTER are to grow up really good friends, tact, wisdom and understanding will be needed all along. Each child must feel fully assured of his niche in the scheme of things; all comparisons must be scrupulously avoided. The aim of the parents should be to feel and express love impartially, but *not* to attempt to treat each child alike, for each is an individual with different needs and reactions. To send a school-boy to bed at the same hour as a toddler for instance, or to give both the same amount of pocket money, would be quite obviously unwise. The principle of distinguishing between the needs of the children at their different stages of development should be remembered all along.

Quarrels will occur even in the best regulated families, but will pass as quickly as April showers if rightly handled, so that no sense of injustice is left behind. The children should settle their tiffs themselves whenever possible, for the fault is usually in some degree on both sides. Mother may come in at the tail end of a scuffle and pounce on Tom for being unkind to 'poor little Jane' without realizing the highly provocative pinpricks the same Jane has been quietly administering!

To separate the contestants without taking sides, and to change the atmosphere by a happy suggestion of a new occupation, is very often sufficient. Then, when each is relaxed at night, a friendly little chat may help to make it easier in future for the older to practise tolerance, forbearance and self-control; and for the younger to be less thoughtless, demanding and cheeky. These bedtime chats should always be with one child at a time and are a very important part of good parenthood. The child who is sure of a fair hearing and a kindly understanding is set free to feel more generous and good-humoured himself, and thus more ready to turn the other cheek.

Brothers and Sisters

THE NEW BABY

While an over-five is nearly always ready to give a rapturous welcome to a new brother or sister, smaller fry are going to find it
very hard to share mother's lap and time without feeling dispossessed. The right introduction is a big help, and in talking about
'his' baby brother or sister we can suggest many happy thoughts
and ideas. These should, however, as far as possible, be based on
reality. It is wise to try and let a child get some idea what a young
baby is like and what he needs. Some children get the impression
that they are going to be presented with a glorified doll, or ready-
made playmate, and feel badly let down by a newcomer who seems
to them merely rather a spoil sport.

For a first introduction the new baby should be in his cradle and
mother's arms and lap empty for the toddler. She should not
expect him to share her wonderful joy, nor should she expatiate too
warmly on the blueness of baby's eyes, the pearliness of his ears,
the downiness of his head, or whatever it may be! The older child,
probably still thoroughly self-centred, interprets such praise to his
own belittling and queries whether *his* eyes, ears, and hair are quite
up to standard!

To enlist the child as a lieutenant in some capacity, and to give
him something new to love and fresh to do, are the best ways of
helping him to adjust to the new situation. A little girl will adore
having a doll to bath, dress and feed. A small boy may enjoy a
panda in the same rôle, or he may be ready for a live pet.

Incidentally, try and turn the warning or reproving 'Don't make
a noise or you'll waken baby'; or 'No, I can't look at your picture
now, I must put baby to bed', or whatever it may be, into something more positive. Love grows through happy experiences; it
won't necessarily exist just because of the blood relationship.

JEALOUSY AND RIVALRY

Parents will often be needed to act as buffers protecting the
children from each other when necessary—particularly the older
children from the depredations of the toddler—and giving each his
own status. It is easy to do this with the eldest, whose privileges and
responsibilities are plain, and with the youngest who often tends

to get spoilt. It is the middle members of the family who may tend to feel inferior. 'What Katy Did at Home and at School' describes very vividly some of the problems of a family hierarchy.

Some mothers are ready to congratulate themselves that all has gone so smoothly that no jealousy exists. Unless there is a gap of at least five years between the children, this is very rare indeed. There may be little jealousy while baby sleeps his days away, but there is almost bound to be some when he begins to take the centre of the nursery stage.

Manifestations of jealousy are so varied that they are not always recognized. Not all children show it openly. In some it takes the form of over-demonstrative affection towards baby. This may be partly due to a desire to win mother's approbation and keep in the limelight; partly to the satisfaction of a bear-hug which can always become a little tighter! Partly, too, of course, to genuine affection.

With some children there is a tendency to regress and behave in babyish ways—to crawl and wet and want to suck the bottle, or be fed at meals. In some it takes the form of tantrums, aggressive or destructive behaviour, disturbed sleep and nightmares.

When parents recognize it, they should seek to be careful to show the extra loving reassurance for which the child is craving, to do all they can to give him back that lost sense of security and stability which baby is challenging. They must never scold, as this adds fuel to the strong emotional feelings by making the child feel he is quite out of favour and is being thoroughly bad.

A friendship between brothers and sisters can be one of the finest relationships in life, so it's worth taking great care to minimize rivalry and help each to enjoy the presence of the others in the home.

XXXIX

DEVELOPING SOCIALLY

To GET ON well with other people, to like and be liked—such an asset throughout life—has roots formed in the earliest nursery days.

The new-born baby is completely non-social. No blandishments will charm him, no frowning faces dismay him. But impressions are being stored in the sub-conscious part of his memory, relating to the handling and management he receives, which will tend to colour all his future outlook. Bit by bit, as his intelligence wakens and his powers of hearing and seeing mature, a baby begins consciously to appreciate the difference between companionship and solitude, and definitely to prefer the former.

As early as two months he watches people, or 'takes notice', as we say; and as he gets older he is often so interested in their doings that he may even forget to suck, if activity is going on around him at feeding-times.

At three months, or earlier, he stops crying at the sound of a friendly voice. At four months he is observant enough to distinguish between faces and will often stare soberly at a stranger, reserving his vivid smile for his friends. Once he has begun to note facial expression there is always the chance that any strangeness in appearance may alarm him; though, as a rule, he is content to go from lap to lap without demur until he is about seven months old. He then begins to roughly divide his world into beloveds, possibles, and strangers. An unaccustomed face may fill him with such a mixture of feeling cheated and of alarm that he may burst into tears!

From now on the rôle of mere observer no longer contents him; he wants to be included in what's afoot. Gradually he begins to mimic, or imitate facial expressions, gestures, emotions, and words. By the time he is nine months, his sociability has developed to the extent of offering rusks or toys to those he trusts, pulling their clothing to attract their attention, babbling to them, and so on.

If in infancy and toddlerdom the child has felt happy and secure; if, as he grows, his relationship to Mother and Daddy, brothers and sisters is well adjusted, then he is strengthened to face the less sympathetic and more challenging contacts with the folk he must meet outside the family circle.

At about a year he dimly recognizes his own self-identity—a nucleus, as it were, of a growing sense of personality. But even at 18 months he is still self-engrossed, and does not realize that others are individuals like himself and with similar feelings.

A big step forward is made round about two years old. The child can now distinguish fairly clearly between things and persons; between himself and others. He names himself when he sees himself in the mirror, whereas before he thought he saw another child. He likes to have another toddler around, but not actually to play with him or to share his toys—so much a part of his own personality at that age.

Parallel Play

All through the third year parallel play is very satisfying to little ones, and if possible duplicate toys should be provided. Social contact may be made crudely enough by pushing, snatching, or even hitting, and these early signs of experimental interest should not be too strongly discouraged. Month by month, if there has been no scolding and badgering, social relations will gradually improve and a rudimentary sense of co-operation and understanding of the rights and feelings of others be achieved. By three years the average child is ready to join a play group or nursery school for a few hours each day with real benefit.

Companionship

Many children feel so strongly the urge to find companionship at this age that they may wander away from home if it is not provided for them. Or they may become unduly clinging and possessive of mother. From now on playmates should be as near the child's own level of development as possible. He who plays only with children older or younger than himself may be feeling he cannot cope with his contemporaries—seeking the company of older children, because they tend to make allowances for him, or give him special protection. Or migrating to the younger ones whom he can boss and care for. That level give-and-take, on which mature, happy mutual relationships depend, is not being really fostered.

Learning how to mix happily with others is the most important of all pre-school lessons. Not to feel others to be much more, or

much less, wonderful than oneself. Neither desiring to push, nor submitting to being pushed. Not getting delirious with excitement, nor trying to hide away. Being able both to get one's own way, or give it up, without generating too much emotional feeling. A mother or teacher-umpire, to tactfully guide, can help so much in these matters.

The Invisible Friend

Quite a number of children round about three create an 'invisible friend'—a sort of 'other self'. He is tremendously real to them and should be treated seriously; there should be no hint of ridicule or disbelief. If the invisible friend is around too much, it is usually a sign that the child is somewhat lonely. If 'he' always behaves remarkably well, it is often a sign the child has feelings of guilt. If 'he' behaves atrociously, it may mean that the child is rebelling inwardly, at being handled too strictly. Wise parents will make the necessary adjustments to help the little one to be at peace with himself and his world; then, as he grows, the 'friend' will gradually fade, usually vanishing altogether about the sixth birthday.

Transition

If his development is good, in the transition from the pre-social to a more social stage at about three, the child gradually becomes more detached from the mother. He also shows feelings of pity, sympathy, modesty, shame and so on, instead of being the amoral and 'cold-blooded' little creature he once was.

By three and a half a child should feel secure enough and trustful enough to be able to share his possessions off and on. By four he often feels protective towards smaller fry; and by five he has mastered some elements of consideration for others, and even developed the rudiments of tact! Any attempt to rush his progress, by expecting an old head on young shoulders; or undue protectiveness, holding him back from experimental overtures, may do harm.

The Gang Age

The gang or herd stage starts round about the age of seven. From now on the child should increasingly identify himself with contemporaries, and be less dependent on the adults. He copies his group slavishly and their good opinion is of the greatest importance to him. This gang age reaches its height at about the age of 11 and is a really necessary part of training for citizenship. From it emerge the later ties of loyalty to mate, country, or Church. Thus wise parents respect the child's loyalty to his gang and never expect, or allow, him to tell tales about its members. But they are wiser still if they seek to satisfy the gregarious instinct by inviting friends into the garden and to tea; also arranging for the child to attend a well-run Sunday school; and linking him or her on to Wolf Cubs or Brownies, or other organizations where hooliganism is not rife, and where standards of conduct and speech are reasonably high.

Playmates

The question of the rough playmate is a tricky one for many parents. Is the undesirable child next door—with his bad speech and unpleasant manners—better than no playmate at all? Is the tough, uncouth guy, on whom your son looks as a hero, to be avoided or cultivated?

Speaking very generally, it seems best that all play should be unobtrusively supervised until a child is, say, three and a half to four years. By that time he will have absorbed the family spirit and code to such an extent that he will not come to too much harm if he is exposed fairly freely to children of a lower standard. We can't keep our children in glass-houses and we must let them find their own level. Along with the rough ways the child will probably learn a lot from the so-called hooligan that is good and fine too. The story of Tom Brown's pre-school days is a good illustration of this.

Odd Man Out

A far more worrying problem is the child who isn't accepted by any group but who always feels 'odd man out'. That is why care must be taken not to sap a child's sense of self-confidence or to lower his self-respect and sense of being worth-while. It's done so easily by constant carping and criticizing; by snubbing when he's at the normal showing-off stage; by comparing him with some other child to his detriment; by assuring him that if he does this or that no one will like him; or by letting him feel dispossessed when the new baby comes to the home. How can a child feel friendly and expect friendliness from others if at home he's constantly told what a little nuisance he is; or if he has a false sense of his value by receiving too much attention from adults?

It is important, too, that the child does not develop any sense that he is 'different' from others from the early days when he is beginning to recognize himself as a person. The little boy with long curls; the little girl with all the wrong clothes; the little school-boy dressed in corduroy when flannel is *de rigeur*; the child who can't join in what's afoot because he hasn't got the same sort of toys or tools as the other children have—these things must be avoided if it is at all possible.

The Only Child

The only child labours under a big handicap in this matter of learning to fit into a group and to feel he really belongs. Children need constant opportunities of seeing their acts mirrored in the reactions of their contemporaries if they are to develop a sympathetic fellow-feeling and a good, intuitive, social approach.

A child needs to discover what does and what does not work or go down with his contemporaries, and to practise his wit or his exploits without being thought a little wonder. He can't develop self-reliance and self-confidence if he plays only with dream children or with grown-ups. He can't get to know himself and recognize his own individuality and powers if he measures himself only against the giant adult, or the obliging teddy bear. He's got to use another child as a yard-stick. He can't harness impulses to be aggressive, or destructive, or to show off, unless, through group play he can find out what the aggressions and boastings of others feel like, and how his contemporaries react to such things.

The younger a child buys his social experiences the less they cost in the long run, and he will accept a criticism from another child better than from an adult. 'You are a baby!' says three-year-old Arthur scornfully, to four-year-old Tom, crying over a scratched knee, and Tom quickly dries up. Had his mother said the same thing, it would have been an added grievance, and his howls would have been redoubled!

Quarrels will be frequent and friendships fleeting in the early experimental days, and tactful adult umpiring often needed. It's important to avoid too much taking of sides, too much moralizing, or 'righteous' indignation. Let the children settle their own score as far as possible, while conscious of a friendly, understanding backing—a friendliness which is extended to the so-called 'enemy' as well as towards the little son or daughter. The power to see the other fellow's point of view, to put oneself in someone else's shoes, is of the greatest value. Giving and taking, leading and following, are lessons only learnt in free group play and best learnt in the three-to-five stage.

Pleasant social manners are a useful asset, but it is a mistake to associate the coming of a visitor with getting uncomfortably scrubbed up; with remembering to use the right hand; to open doors, and so on. Friendliness should come from the heart, and spontaneous expressions of it, however unconventional, are to be preferred to forced and insincere ones. A shy child will enjoy and benefit from games of tea-parties, acting host, and so on, and, given a little help of this kind will feel more at ease and less awkward, and thus in time better able to enjoy a visitor's presence.

Paying visits to other houses is good if enjoyed; but 'a party' with its dressing up, and instructions as to behaviour, fills many a child with real alarm. Watching the happiness of other children in a small class for eurythmics, or dancing, is a useful preparation for school life, but any urging a child to join in, or any showing disapproval if he retreats from friendly advances, will only increase the original reluctance.

It is so worth while taking time and trouble to help a child to feel increasingly at home with others, and to gradually find his niche in the community with confidence and enjoyment.

FOR FURTHER READING

Natural Development of the Child, by Agatha Bowley. E. and S. Livingstone, 8s. 6d.

The Spirit of the Child, by Marjorie Thornburn. Allen & Unwin, 3s. 6d.

Points for Parents, by Lady Pakenham. Wedenfeld & Nicolson, 10s. 6d.

XL

SPIRITUAL DEVELOPMENT

NO BOOK ON babies growing up would be complete without some comment—however inadequate—on the needs of the child's spirit, as distinct from his soul and body.

All laws of growth and development are very similar, and if neglected or ignored, stunting is inevitable. To apply those relating to the spirit is harder for most of us, for we have more personal experience of the nurture of the body, or the mind, than we have of the nurture of the spirit. Religious ideals are best caught rather than taught, so pity the child born to parents to whom the things of the spirit are a sealed book.

How can a child's spirit be nurtured? First of all it needs good *air*. Parents who themselves have a spiritual awareness of the Presence of God, and the power of prayer, unconsciously create an atmosphere in which a child's spirit can thrive, and in which the heaven which 'lay about him in his infancy' does not altogether 'fade into the light of common day'. They will have prayed for him before birth; and by his cradle throughout his unconscious infant days; so, as he grows and begins to talk, it is not difficult for them to convey to the child something of the joyous wonder and love which they themselves experience.

Then the spirit needs *food*, and this, as St. Peter tells us, is chiefly 'the sincere milk of the Word'. All children love stories, and when they ask for them are in a receptive mood, open to receive many helpful suggestions. The Bible is a wonderful store-house of stories which reveal God and His relations with man, and, with a little time and trouble in learning the art of telling such stories, or through using well-expressed books, children can have this food for their spirits from quite an early age.

Little children love repetition and at first the same story can be told again and again. As they grow older, and especially round about eight years, when the powers of memorizing are specially good, the habit of 'hiding God's word in the heart' by learning a weekly portion is a splendid plan. A famous head-mistress has said that she could never be too thankful that her parents insisted on her learning the Collect by heart each Sunday. At the time it was a grind, but it has proved a life-long possession. Children will enjoy collecting illustrated texts, just as they do cigarette cards; the lovely words sown in their minds, perhaps not understood at the time, will often come back to them in times of stress in later life.

Then the spirit needs *sunshine*. Pity a child to whom religion is something forbidding; to whom God is a Policeman rather than a Dear Companion and Saviour. The wise mother feeds her child's spirit with the beauty of God's creation, helps him to thank God for all the simple pleasures of his day, and does not expect from him a religious precocity which could only do harm. The right pictures to illustrate Bible stories or hymns, are so important that too much care cannot be taken in choosing them, for the vivid impression they make is often lasting, for good or ill.

Then the spirit needs *exercise*. This includes a gradual appreciation of the difference between right and wrong, good and evil—through stories, through wise correcting of faults, and through helpful example. And a chance to put into action some spiritual lesson learnt—loving one's neighbour in some practical way; turning the other cheek; denying oneself or whatever it may be.

Forming Habits

Some parents, hardly distinguishing between the growth of the spirit and the acquiring of certain religious tenets, say 'Oh, wait until he is older and can choose for himself!' Not only does this mean that without the spiritual vitamins it needs the spirit is inevitably dwarfed; but, as Nature abhors a vacuum, the child's instinct to worship will be turned into other channels, if not shown the way to love and worship God.

Again, we must remember that 'habit is ten natures', as Charlotte Mason of the P.N.E.U. used to say. A pattern of behaviour is being built day by day and it should include the experience of simple thanksgiving, confession, and petition to God, before the day starts and before going to sleep, as surely as teeth-brushing and hand-washing. The moment's pause to say a grace, may only be a form at times, but it is a recognition of dependence on God, highly satisfying to the enquiring child, and a family tradition well worth cultivating.

Of course a child will not always feel like saying his prayers or his grace, or going to Sunday School. It would be a mistake to have any sort of force or compulsion in such matters, but usually the atmosphere can be changed by a tactful approach. Children love to dramatize themselves and, after about the age of six, the idea of being a soldier prepared to fight and to do right, even when it is very hard, will be a real help to them.

Saying grace

Children's Questions

Parents are often perplexed by their children's question 'What is God like?' 'Why don't the stars fall out of the sky?' 'What happens when I die?' 'Are there really angels?' In teaching the 'facts of life' modern parents recognize how wrong it would be to put a child off by fairy stories, and how necessary it is to be sure of the facts and to know how to pass them on in appropriate language. It is equally important for them to take trouble to study the revelation of God as revealed in the Bible, and to get their own ideas clarified so that, with humility and reverence, when the child asks for spiritual bread, they do not offer him a materialistic stone. Alas! for all the help they get in these matters, many children might well be described as spiritual orphans.

It is sad if key words, which will be used in expressing the things of God, convey unhappy or frightening ideas. This is especially so where the word 'Father' is concerned. Will it conjure up a picture of someone strong, brave, gentle, loving, compassionate—or someone self-indulgent, irritable, brusque and stern?

Parents Responsibility
It is said that if a child has never worshipped his mother he never will be able to worship any Deity. Whether this is true or no, the responsibility of the parents is very great. It is useless for them to exhort their child to show qualities of goodwill, peaceableness, honesty, sincerity, or whatever it may be, if their own lives do not display these virtues. 'What you are speaks so loud I cannot hear what you say,' is a remark to ponder.

A spirit of reverence is more easily acquired by watching Mummy and Daddy kneel and close their eyes, than it is through exhortations from watchful parents. In fact, the best way for a child to learn to pray is to listen to his parent praying simply to God, or singing the hymns which have been beloved of generations of little ones.

In the appendix below books which may help are given. This slight chapter is just a plea for a recognition of the needs of the child's spirit and a reminder of how, left unnurtured, warping must surely follow.

FOR FURTHER READING

The Christian Household, by Anne Proctor. Longmans, Green, 2*s*.
The Children's Faith, by Phyllis Ingram-Johnson. S.P.C.K., 4*s*.
Sunday to Sunday with the Under Fives, by Nancy Quayle. S.P.C.K., 4*s*. 6*d*.
Beryl and Derek's Bible Treasury. Shaw Picture Co., 3, Creed Lane, London, E.C., 2*s*. 6*d*. paper, 10*s*. 6*d*. cloth.
The Tuck Me Up Book, by Lettice Bell, Parts I and II, 3*s*.
A for Angel, by Joan Gale Thomas. Mowbrays, 4*s*. 6*d*.
My Own Picture Hymn Book. S.C.M. Press Limited, 3*s*. 6*d*.
Tender Shepherd, First Prayers. Samuel Bagster, 6*d*.
Train Up a Child, by E. W. Crabb, Dip.Th., Dip.Litt. Paternoster Press, 6*s*.

XLI

THE HANDICAPPED CHILD

A PROPORTION OF each generation of children have some handicap in life; they may be born with it, or it may follow some accident or illness.

No matter what the handicap is, whether connected with the brain, the senses, or the limbs, there is always much that can be done to make life easier for the child, even if the condition itself may not be amenable to treatment.

The first essential is a good diagnosis, and parents should not shy away from facing any unpalatable fact, but, with an expert's help, try and assess, as dispassionately as possible, the realities of the situation.

If the trouble is curable, the sooner it is tackled, while growth is still rapid, bones still forming and habits not yet set, the better. If it is not curable, the sooner the child and the family come to terms with it, the easier it will be to find ways of compensating for it, leading to a measure of happiness and usefulness.

The child with a mental defect has to be patiently taught to do things which the average child would pick up automatically, and great care in avoiding bad, anti-social habits must be taken. The child who cannot see, has to learn about his world through touch, and be trained to be self-reliant and independent.

Care should in all cases be taken to assess what the child's potentials really are so that he is not discouraged by being given tasks beyond him; nor left unchallenged and unstimulated by having everything done for him.

The parents' attitude is, of course, most important. It must not be too emotional; it must not weaken the child by over-protecting, over-pitying. Equally it must be steadily and sympathetically loving and understanding, or the child will feel rejected and inferior. Any personal feelings of shame or failure must be resolutely overcome, and the child drawn into normal activities and companionships as far as it is at all possible.

In all training or treatment the child must be an active partner and his reactions be carefully studied, so that an environment which suits him can be planned.

Though it is hard at first for parents to accept that his own child has some defect, yet many of these children bring special love and happiness with them; and many, in the end, lead wonderfully full and happy lives, amply repaying all the devoted care given in the early years.

Some addresses, where special help for many types of handicapped children is available, and books or pamphlets which deal with their needs are listed below:

FOR FURTHER READING AND SOME HELPFUL ADDRESSES

The Backward Child

National Association for the Parents of Backward Children, 84–86, Chancery Lane, London, W.C.2.

National Association for Maternity and Child Welfare Centres, 5, Tavistock Place, London, W.C.1.

National Association for Mental Health, 39, Queen Anne Street, London, W.1.

Opening Doors, from N.A.M.C.W.C., 9d. plus postage.

Children who can Never go to School, from N.A.M.H., 6d. plus postage.

The Retarded Child, by Herta Loewry. The Staples Press (Guide to Parents, 10s. 6d.; abridged edition, 3s. 6d.).

For the Parents of a Mongol Child, from Sunfield Children's Homes, Clent, Stourbridge, Worcs., 1s.

The Story of a Backward Child, by Marjorie Shave. Independent Press, 6d.

The Child Who Never Grew, by Pearl S. Buck. Methuen & Co., Ltd., 5s.

Asthma

The Research Council, King's College, London, W.C.2.

The Handicapped Child

Physical Exercises for Asthma. H. K. Lewis, Ltd., 2s. 2d.

The Asthmatical Child, by John Wright. Simpkin Marshall, 2s. 6d.

Blindness

The Royal National Institute for the Blind (N.I.B.), 224–6, Great Portland Street, London, W.1.

Care of Young Blind Children. 6d.

Cripples

Central Council for the Care of Cripples, 34, Eccleston Square, London, S.W.1.

Mrs. Estrid Dane,
   Neumann-Neurode Clinic, 2, Holland Park Avenue, London, W.11.

Deafness

The Deaf Children's Association, 1, Macklin Street, London, W.C.2.

If Your Child is Deaf. 6d.

Epilepsy

British Epilepsy Association, 136, St. George Street, London, W.1

Children With Epilepsy. 3d.

Social Aspects of Epilepsy. 9d.

Spastics

National Spastics Society, 44, Stratford Road, London, W.8.

British Council for the Welfare of Spastics, 26, Cranleigh Parade, Limpsfield Road, Sanderstead.

The Brain Injured Child. Obtainable from the Sunfield Children's Home, Clent, Worcester, 1s. 9d.

The Handicapped Child, by Karl Konig. New Knowledge Books, 1s. 6d.

XLII

NERVOUS HABITS

TRICKS AND HABITS, which give comfort and satisfaction to a little child but are worrying for the parents, often develop in early days and wisdom is needed in dealing with them. The direct attack on any habit is almost always unwise, but ways of gently discouraging, while providing an alternative outlet for repressed energies and tensions, can be very helpful.

Remember quite little children want to 'get control' over their adults and will repeat a trick which makes them feel important because it leads to an emotional stir on the parents' part. A few of the more usual comfort habits are discussed below, and other variants need much the same sort of treatment.

Thumb-sucking. At first the mouth is highly sensitive and baby will bring everything to it. He will be specially mouth-conscious, too, while teething, and will tend to return to the infantile comfort habit in later childhood when unhappy. To gently discourage the habit we must see that baby gets enough legitimate sucking exercise —15–20 minutes at feed, five times a day; hard toys and food on which to champ and bite, and lots to do with the hands. Boredom, jealousy, anxiety, must be dealt with at the appropriate levels. If baby falls asleep with his thumb in his mouth, the mother should quietly remove it and prop up his chin so that mouth-breathing is avoided. The wearing of loose, cotton gloves, or a thumb-stall, may act as a mild deterrent if put on without comment, or as part of a game.

Nail-biting may have its roots in inner resentments and unexpressed aggression. We can help by patience and love, and by giving the child satisfactions of a creative character. Keeping the cuticles well oiled, and wearing gloves at night will help, also a good manicure set. Be sure vitamin B is adequate in the diet.

Nervous Habits

Tricks, grimaces, fidgeting habits will be helped by learning how to relax, by extra rest, extra minerals and vitamins in the diet; but not by being told, 'Don't do that!' 'You are too big now', or 'No one will love you!'

Masturbation should be treated on a par with speaking with the mouth full, or other undesirable ways of behaviour. For fuller discussion see p. 180. With an older child the trouble is often bound up with a difficulty in making friendly relations and going outward to others, and here is where help is needed.

Head-banging may start from some discomfort in the ears, but if the child gets pleasure from it, it tends to be repetitive. In some cases it has its roots in the unconscious desire to punish, or be punished. Pad the head of the cot to prevent injury. Clamp the cot down so that the child cannot get satisfaction from rocking it. See that bedtime rituals are soothing and happy ones. Provide outlets for using up aggressive feelings.

Bed-wetting. Most children are able to keep the bed dry by the time they are three, though they may still need a little help in attending to themselves. Encourage self-help and, as a rule, do not let the child get into the habit of passing water while still asleep, or he may continue to do this. A torch under the pillow, and a light untensil handy, will help.

If bed-wetting persists, check on various points of management. Too-concentrated urine makes the bladder irritable, so be sure the child is drinking enough fluid in the early part of the day. Query worms, acid urine, or some urinary infection. See that the foreskin is not tight, and the parts kept clean.

The bedroom should be well ventilated, the child cosily warm, but not over-hot or stuffy. Muscular development should be encouraged by an active life, cold sponging, etc.

The trouble is quite often emotional, rather than physical, due to various stresses and strains, and may be associated with nightmares. Happy, encouraging handling, which bolsters up the child's self-respect and sense of all being well, will help. It should be taken for granted that he wants a dry bed, and that he will soon have one, suggestion being used positively to give extra confidence. Raising the foot of the bed on blocks; giving salt in a final drink;

arousing half an hour earlier than usual; providing new pyjamas, have all been known to work. Study the individual child and be sure he is getting plenty of vitamins and minerals in his diet.

FOR FURTHER READING

Children's Fears. N.A.M.H., 1s. 4½d.
The Nervous Child, by H. C. Cameron. Oxford University Press, 12s. 6d.

XLIII

SKIN AFFECTIONS

THE SKIN IS a wonderful structure, which is not only a protective cover to the body, but also an organ by means of which elimination of unwanted by-products takes place. Sweating also helps the body to maintain its even temperature. The care of the skin, which is naturally very delicate at first, is an important part of mothercraft, and is discussed in the chapters on bathing (p. 63) and sunbathing (p. 104).

A few of the more common nursery skin troubles are given here.

Birthmarks

It is said that one baby in every ten is born with some kind of birthmark. Some of these are inherited and apparently due to faults of development in the embryonic stage, before the mother is even aware of her pregnancy.

The four more usual types of birthmarks are: staining, strawberry marks, port-wine marks, and moles. Naturally, a doctor's advice should be sought in regard to any treatment.

Staining, which flushes the middle of the forehead, the eyelids, and the nape of the neck, as a rule disappears entirely a few weeks or months after birth.

The *strawberry mark*, which gets its name from its scarlet colour is often quite small at first, but tends to grow rapidly in the first six months. In practically all cases this disappears spontaneously by the time the child is five or so. Methods used to make it disappear rapidly may leave a permanent mark, so they should not be lightly used.

The port-wine stain does not tend to grow, but unfortunately neither does it fade. It will depend partly on its position whether it should be treated or not, and an expert should be consulted. A cosmetic coverage is sometimes all that is advised.

Moles are dark brown in colour, and may be as small as pin points, or very large; they may be raised or flat. They should be treated early, as they are unlikely to disappear spontaneously, and may increase severely at puberty. Freezing with carbon dioxide snow, or incising surgically, are methods usually advised.

Hives, nettle rash, red gum, urticaria

Types of rashes primarily associated with difficulties of digestion or with over-heating. Their cause should be sought, when cure soon follows. They may appear as minute water-filled blisters, come up as weals, or show as a small diffuse rash of pinkish colour.

A reduction of sugar and starch in the diet; extra water to drink; and care to see that air can circulate freely round the child, that there is no heating rubber under the head, and in hot weather, no wool next the skin, will usually soon clear the condition. Be sure that the bowels are functioning well. Any irritation can be allayed by dabbing the parts with Ponds Extract, or a calamine preparation, or by swabbing with a weak solution of bicarbonate of soda, a small teaspoon to a pint of water. Talcum powder used freely is also helpful.

Buttocks—red or sore

Sore buttocks are often caused by acid motions, or urine, due to an unbalanced diet; or by external irritations due to poor washing of napkins (see p. 156). A damped napkin should never be reapplied, and rinsing should be very thorough. Non-porous pilches should not be worn for long periods.

If the parts are merely red and spotty, dust with a suitable powder (one of equal parts of zinc and starch will do). If the area is scalded, spread a square of gauze with zinc and castor oil ointment, or a calomine preparation and apply; or gently anoint the parts, using a swab of cotton wool, and then lay the gauze square over to protect the napkin.

Exposing the affected part to light and air for considerable periods in a warm atmosphere is a good plan; if the child is happy to lie on his face during part of the time it will be beneficial.

Eczema

There are many kinds of eczema, with many degrees of seriousness, and with any skin outbreak medical advice should be sought. Care must be taken to avoid irritants. Over-heating is one—do not 'toast' baby by the fire, or in the sun. Avoid oppressive coverings and stagnant air. A little shirt of soft muslin or Aertex can be worn next to the skin under a wool vest, and muslin collars and cuffs can be attached to woolly jackets.

The diet must be watched carefully. If breast-fed, the mother must keep sweet and rich foods low, and it is best to do this throughout pregnancy, too. Some babies are allergic to cow's milk —which may be related to the cow's diet. Your doctor may advise a change to goat's milk, nut milk, or the Cow and Gate Allergilac milk, to clear the condition. Evaporated milk mixtures, very easily digested, are sometimes helpful. Vegetable juices should be started early and heating foods be kept low.

Only really soft water should be allowed to touch the skin— boiled rain-water is good. No soap should be used, unless recommended by a doctor. Cleanse the parts gently with liquid medicated paraffin, or an emulsifying lotion, or with normal saline, or boiled milk to which a small pinch of boric acid has been added. Do not use oil, for it prevents the evaporation of sweat and this makes the skin hot and irritable.

To relieve irritation and prevent scratching a soothing ointment will be prescribed, and this may have to be changed from time to time. Steps must be taken to prevent the child rubbing the affected parts, and thus spreading the trouble. Simple splints of corrugated cardboard, covered with soft muslin and tied with tapes, will enable a baby to wave his arms but not to bend them; or cotton or Aertex gloves can be worn, tying above the elbow.

Infantile eczema is usually outgrown during the third year, and its discomfort can be much lessened by careful watching of all circumstances which lead to its aggravation and making wise adjustments. Worry, strain and fatigue will affect the skin at all ages.

Care of Scalp and Hair

It is never wise to let a baby's head get over-hot and his cot should stand well away from the wall so that air may circulate round it freely. His pram hood should be kept down whenever possible.

Any pillow used should be filled with hair, not down or feathers; and head coverings should not be worn unnecessarily, and, when used, must be light, well-ventilated and non-irritating.

Washing

Baby's head is washed daily at first but gradually, as the hair gets thicker, the intervals can be spaced to once a week. Boiled rain-water, or water softened with oatmeal, should be used if possible, with a little pure super-fatted soap. Rinsing should be thorough. Do not be afraid of rubbing over the fontanelle area. If the skin is dry, massage in a little baby cream afterwards.

Baby's brush should be washed frequently and kept covered from dust. It should have long, soft, silky bristles. For the older child a firmer bristle is needed, and the Mason Pearson brush is good. Combs must be used with great care, or they may scratch, and cause irritation. In brushing, turn the hair gently upwards and out-wards away from the scalp. Light massage will promote a flow of blood to the scalp area and thus feeds the hair roots.

Hair should be cut very carefully, tapering, and avoiding too straight a line. Curly hair should be trimmed early, for if allowed to grow heavy the curl will tend to be spoilt. When a child first goes to a hairdresser, care must be taken to see that he enjoys the experience and is not frightened by it. A special children's department is ideal, with toys to catch his interest.

Scurf

Should scurf appear, apply warm, medicated liquid paraffin or olive oil; leave on over-night and, in the morning, wipe the area with cotton-wool dipped in paraffin to which a few drops of thymol have been added. Adults who care for baby should look to their own hair toilet, as the trouble can be contagious.

For an older child troubled with dandruff, wash the head well with green soft soap to which a tablespoon of surgical spirits is added. If the hair is very greasy, it will help to clear the condition if a detergent cream is used for every third shampoo. For normal hair use a cream shampoo or green soft soap. A little lemon juice or vinegar in the final rinsing water, adding a little olive oil if the scalp is dry, will leave the hair soft and silky.

Lice

Children even from good homes may, unfortunately, become infected with head lice if in contact with others with such an infestation. Thus, any child who is scratching the head a great deal should be carefully examined, using a magnifying-glass if available. The thicker and longer the hair the more likely the infection, hence girls are more often troubled than boys.

The female louse—of a greyish, white colour, difficult to distinguish from dandruff—lays many eggs, which she cements firmly to hair shafts. Ordinary combing will not remove these nits, and, left alone, they will soon hatch out into living lice.

To destroy the larvae as well as the living insects is essential. After such destruction, the empty nit shells will continue to stick to the hair unless steps are taken to remove them.

D.D.T. preparations such as Suleo can be used effectively, but, before applying, shampoo the head thoroughly using a carbolic soap, or Derbac. Then, parting the hair well, apply the preparation by means of swabs of cotton-wool, paying particular attention to the nape of the neck and the region of the ears. Leave for 48 hours before again shampooing vigorously. Repeat the treatment at the end of the week for safety's sake.

To remove the nit shells, lather the head well, with a solution of soft soap to which one-third part of crude paraffin (kerosine) has been added. With a fine-tooth comb, or nit comb, remove this lather, and the nits entangled in it will come away.

XLIV

NURSERY AILMENTS

THERE ARE BOUND to be times when the children are out of sorts or suffer from minor disabilities. The following notes may help mothers, both in the realm of prevention and in the use of simple home measures to reinforce the child's own inherent self-healing powers.

Circumcision

A controversial matter with pros and cons and a doctor's advice should be sought. If it is not done there is little need to retract the foreskin, for nature has her own plans of developing the prepuce, which is close fitting at first. When the child is about three he can be taught to clean the area occasionally in his bath, much as he cleans his ears, with a little soapy water.

Diarrhoea

In infancy diarrhoea may be due to over-feeding; to contaminated food; to a chill; or to a definite germ. Scrupulous cleanliness regarding baby's food is essential and milk should be kept as cool as possible as bacteria flourish in warmth.

If the stools are loose, green and watery, frequent and perhaps excessive, a doctor should at once be consulted. Meanwhile it will be wise to give drinks of plain boiled water only for 12 to 24 hours, depending on the degree of the trouble. Milk should be reintroduced cautiously, using a fat-free mixture and making it only a third- to half-strength to begin with, slowly working back to normal.

A baby with diarrhoea should be kept warm, particularly over the abdomen and feet. Soiled napkins should be put straight into a pail with a disinfectant such as Dettol, and boiled before re-use. Bottles and teats should be thoroughly boiled.

Earache

This may be serious and if there is any discharge (not the normal wax), or any redness behind the ears, consult a doctor at once. Warmth can be soothing, such as a thinly filled and covered hot-water-bottle. Lay the child on the bad side, to let any discharge come away. Do not attempt to syringe without advice.

Knock Knee

If the heavy baby takes his body weight too soon, or if the diet has lacked vitamin D, there is a risk of the ligaments of the knee joint becoming lax. If the line of the knee is wrong it will affect the arch and stance of the foot.

If the degree of the trouble is marked an orthopedic specialist should be consulted. (See pp. 125–127 for preventive measures.)

Hiccups

Young babies are often troubled with these and particularly after they have brought up wind: To offer a little boiled water in tiny sips, to encourage him to swallow frequently, may help. If very troublesome, lie him over a warm hot-water bottle on your lap, and gently rub the back upwards. With an older child slow deep breathing helps, especially breathing in and out of a brown paper bag, which will contain carbon dioxide from previous expirations, and thus make the breathing deeper. Hiccups are caused by a spasm of the diaphragm, or the irritation of some part of the nervous system affecting this muscle, and changes in posture are often beneficial.

Rupture

The protrusion of underlying tissue through a weak spot in the outer wall is termed a rupture and occurs most commonly near the navel (umbilical) or in the groin (inguinal). In both cases spontaneous recovery is probable if the child's all-round development is good. To give a support which makes the muscles of the area flabby tends to handicap. A doctor's advice should be sought.

Tummy-ache

All pain has a cause and this should be quietly sought. Tummy-ache, like many other kinds of pains, may be due to a number of possible causes. Indiscretion at meals; constipation; swallowed catarrh, are frequent causes. A dislike of school, or whatever comes next on the programme, gives an uneasy feeling in the pit of the stomach, and unconsciously is used as a way of escape. The start of many illnesses leads to an upset tummy. Infections of the urine also cause abdominal pain, as do infected stomach glands; so if tummy-aches recur persistently, report to your doctor, keeping a watch for other symptoms to help in a proper diagnosis.

Worms

The eggs of thread worms may be found in house dust, on food, in coats of animals, on towels, or on toilet seats used by someone already infected. They are usually conveyed by the child's hands to the mouth and then swallowed. If the intestines are thoroughly healthy, the eggs may not hatch out; if the diet is poorly balanced and the child having a lot of sweet stuff, they are more likely to do so. It may be as much as 28 days before a fully grown female worm emerges and lays her eggs—which will run into thousands—outside the anus. Irritations round the area leads to scratching and then to reinfection via the nails and mouth. Preventive hygienic measures are thus as important as any direct attack.

Preventive Measures. Be sure each child has his own toilet arrangements. Use stout brown paper on lavatory seats. See that each scrubs nails and hands after use of toilet and before meals. The child should wear closed cotton knickers, or sleeping-suits, or cotton gloves. Boil these daily. Use plenty of soap, water and sunlight in the home.

In cooking meat or fish, beware of rapid sealing of the outside so that the centres are inadequately sterilized. Wash green vegetables well and soak in salted water before cooking. Carefully separate all surfaces of saladings and wash under a running tap. Root vegetables, if eaten raw, should be dipped in boiling water for 30–60 seconds after thorough cleansing.

Treatment. Your doctor will probably recommend a vermicide with a piperazine base which will be quickly effective, but because of the risk of any eggs hatching out it will be a good plan to gently cleanse the skin all around the anus at night, using cotton-wool dipped in liquid paraffin, or witch hazel. Then apply a thick disinfectant ointment. Remove this carefully in the morning, wiping gently away from the opening. Be sure to scrub your hands afterwards.

Where medical advice is not readily available, the use of a little flowers of sulphur, as much as will go on a sixpence, twice daily for five days might be tried. Garlic is also helpful.

Beware of treatments which upset and worry a child. These will do much more harm than the parasite itself. Give the treatment without telling a young child the reason why, as many children are really upset by the knowledge. If you can prevent reinfection by careful attention to the hygiene, the cure will work much faster.

CARE IN SICKNESS

When a child seems out of sorts it is often wise to isolate him, in case he is about to develop an infectious illness. By putting him to bed his body gets extra rest, which helps the fight against any infection, while there will be less risk of chilling. The bedroom should be bright and well aired, and happy occupations arranged so that the child does not fret but quite enjoys his temporary banishment.

His mother's attitude is very important, for the more poorly the child the more suggestible he will become. Over-solicitude on her part will make him feel worse; but he does need a warm, secure feeling of being specially cared for. It is usually a mistake to question him about his aches and pains. By gestures and odd remarks he will soon reveal where the trouble lies and more accurately than in a verbal response which is often misleading.

Even if he does not seem feverish the temperature should be taken—and if it is found to be raised only fluid should be given for the next meal. The temperature should be taken again within three hours and diet regulated accordingly (see p. 215).

If the tongue is white, and the child has a running nose, or a sore throat, no milk should be included in the fluids, which should be plain water, lemon and barley, and other fruit drinks; also the juices from raw and cooked vegetables, diluted and flavoured with a little Marmite or Vecon, etc.

If the stools are loose, apple juice and grated apple pulp are specially helpful. If there is constipation, a little magnesia or fruit salt can be added to one of the drinks.

A sick child should be kept cosily warm but not be oppressed with clothes. A light sweater, or loosely-knitted bed-jacket will be helpful. It should have long sleeves to allow him to play with books or toys without getting chilled.

The skin will give off many poisons during an illness, and to help this a certain amount of initial sweating is good. Afterwards the child must be washed down well all over, or given a bath if he is well enough. He should then be put into fresh, well-aired garments, and clothing regulated carefully.

If the feet are cold, loose bed-socks will be helpful, or a very well-covered hot-water bottle. With a very young child this should go under the mattress, or between blankets, so that there is no possibility of a burn.

A clean mouth is important, both to avoid swallowing poisons, and to prevent tooth decay. A mouth-wash before meals, and cleaning the teeth after them, is ideal.

Glare on the eyes must be avoided, a light screen being helpful, so that the room can be bright but the child's eyes protected. This can also be used to cut off draughts, while keeping the room airy.

Temperature Taking

A good clinical thermometer should be kept in the house and the child's temperature taken when he is out of sorts. If it rises much over 100° F. a doctor should be notified. Always shake it down well to about 96° F. before using. To shake down, grasp firmly by end opposite to the bulb and use a sharp outward motion of the wrist

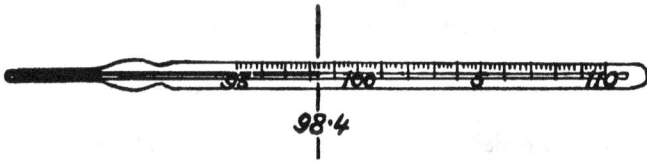

98·4

with an abrupt stop—like cracking a whip. It is wise to do this over a soft surface when practising!

Do not take the temperature in the mouth after hot or cold food has been taken until at least a quarter of an hour has elapsed. If the child is too young to place the thermometer under the tongue without biting on it, it can often be slid gently along the floor of the right cheek, the child being told he is 'smoking a cigarette'. If there is feverishness the mercury will rise rapidly in the first 30 seconds.

In the groin, or under the arm-pit, the temperature reading is obtained much more slowly, and will be lower than the mouth reading. At least five minutes will be necessary to obtain a reliable result.

The temperature is highest in the rectum, but this method is only suitable for the young and placid baby and should not normally be used. Always write a temperature down and do not trust to memory. The younger the child, the less stable is the heat-regulating mechanism; thus a high temperature may have comparatively little significance.

Colds, Coughs, Catarrhs

The main causes of colds are (1) direct infection, (2) chilling or wetting, (3) a blood-stream laden with impurities.

Little ones should not be taken to places where infection is likely to be present; and anyone with a cold should keep at a respectful distance. If the mother catches a cold she should gargle, scrub her nails, and put on a clean overall before attending to baby or his food. To wear a mask of four to six thicknesses of gauze, or a large handkerchief folded into a triangle, to cover nose and mouth, is an added precaution. A useful mask can be made from gauze, a yard long by 6 in. wide. Fold into four lengthways, and machine down three sides, leaving one side (9 in. in length) open. Slip a piece of soft paper, or thin lint, between the gauze layers. Tack tapes to the four corners, and fit the mask, adjusting the tapes, before stitching these firmly, to ensure a comfortable fit over nose and mouth.

A small clean square of linen should be pinned to baby's dress each day so that there will be no temptation to use an adult handkerchief. Older children should be provided with clean rags, or paper handkerchiefs, and be trained to use once only, and then to burn, or put into a covered receptacle. Re-using a hankie is a sure way of keeping up a cold, while pockets soon become highly infected.

Because dust and germs in the air find lodgement in the nasal cavities these should be emptied regularly. The small baby should be encouraged to sneeze, and the toddler trained to blow his nose. This must always be done gently, and preferably one nostril at a time. Strong blowing might spread infection to ear passages or the sinuses. All children should be taught to breathe through the hair-lined nose, not through the open mouth.

Chilling

While giving children the benefit of fresh air day and night, they should not be allowed to sleep, sit, or play in a direct draught. Sudden changes in temperature, such as being fed by a warm fire and then going straight out of doors should be avoided. Care must be taken to prevent chilling through being inadequately clothed, especially about the feet or ankles; or by cooling down too quickly after getting hot playing. Clothing should be especially light while the child is active, and an extra garment added when he is sitting still. All clothing should be well aired, including pram mat-tresses and pillows. Shoes for older children should be damp-proof and socks changed daily. General toning measures are good, and the cool sponge can be started with most babies round about six months, while sun and air baths are also very beneficial.

To keep the blood free from toxins, clogging, mucus-forming foods should be kept low, and all those which are devitalized, especially white sugar and sweets. Natural foods, giving jaws and teeth plenty of exercise; and cleansing ones, including salads and fruits, should be provided liberally. The sunshine vitamins must be given regularly (see p. 8). If a cold seems pending, to give two or three meals of vegetable juices and fruit juices only, withholding every other food, helps the body to do its own cleansing.

Simple protective measures that can be tried when infectious con-tacts are unavoidable are the giving of a few drops of Langdale's Essence of Cinnamon in water, or fruit, before the school child sets out; or some onion or garlic juice, both of which it is said help to disinfect the blood-stream. Onion juice is obtainable by slicing an onion, covering with brown sugar or honey, and leaving to stand until the juice runs out and a quite palatable syrup is formed. A spoonful of this can be given on an empty stomach. Deodorised forms of garlic are obtainable.

Treatment for a cold must depend on the age of the child, his general heaith, and what the weather is like. Some colds can be blown or sunned away; with others it is best to have the victim in bed—to give extra rest, to prevent infections being spread, and to keep the body at an even temperature. A really warm bath may be helpful, the general aim being to promote the circulation of the blood, and to encourage elimination, through the pores of the skin, the bowels, the bladder and the nose.

A cold starts in the nose, but may spread down to the throat and the bronchial tubes. Thus at the very onset of a cold it can sometimes be averted by irrigating the nasal passages very very gently. You can use glycerine and thymol (1 in 8); or a very weak solution of salt and water (a saltspoon to a tumblerful), or even a little pure cod-liver oil. Use a sterile fountain-pen filler, or small nasal douche, and have the child with the head well back, downwards and backwards, chin pointing to the ceiling. Insert just a little of the preparation, letting it trickle down at the back of the nose into the mouth; afterwards help the child to blow down well, one nostril at a time. Secretions are thus increased temporarily and the multiplying bacteria at the root of the nose may in this way be greatly reduced. But great care is necessary or infections may be driven into ear passages.

If a baby's nose is very stuffy just before a feed or bedtime, cleanse the lower part of the nostrils gently with twists of cotton-wool dipped in a tumbler of warm water to which half a small teaspoon of salt has been added, or use Nostroline. If breathing is at all distressed, get medical advice at once.

If the throat or chest are affected, try warm compresses round the throat ending with a cold compress. To give these cut a strip of flannel a suitable width. Prepare a solution of 2 tablespoons of commercial Epsom salts to about half a pint of hot water, or use plain hot water. Wring the flannel out well and wrap immediately round the throat, covering with oiled silk to keep in heat and moisture; lightly bandage in place. Remove when the flannel has cooled, repeating once or twice. Then end with a cold compress which can be left on all night if wished. For this, use a strip of linen wrung out of a cold solution, bandaging with flannel.

Rubbing the chest is soothing and brings healing blood to the parts. Use a preparation such as Vick, or a mixture of oils.

When the throat is at all painful, it may help a child to get to sleep if he gargles with hot water containing a crushed aspirin.

It is not really wise to leave a cold to run its course, or to dismiss it lightly as 'only a cold'. It may be the precursor of an infectious illness; it may, wrongly treated or neglected, pave the way for bronchitis and other serious respiratory troubles. By using all the simple home measures at your command the period of discomfort can be reduced to a minimum and the child's resistance built up for the future.

Coughs

Coughs may come from various causes and a doctor should usually be consulted. Cold air will often start up a cough, so it may be necessary to keep some heating going through the night. Dry air will have a similar effect, so to have a kettle simmering may be necessary to moisten the atmosphere. Some forms of cough can be nursed on a balcony; others require such an even temperature that it may be necessary to shut the window and open the door at night.

Inhaling

If your doctor advises inhaling, great care must be taken that there is no chance of child scalding himself or upsetting the fluid. An earthenware jar, warmed, and then having about an inch of boiling water and ½ teaspoon of Friar's Balsam added will do very well, replenishing if necessary as the steam gets less. Or an earthenware teapot can be used, not quite half filled with boiling water and a small teaspoon of the tincture of benzoin. Wrap it up well to keep in warmth and prevent scalding and let the child inhale the steam from the spout. If a 'tent' or cover is needed, it should be of some transparent, light material, so that the child does not feel worried and oppressed. Presented as an interesting plan, most children enjoy inhaling and find it a great relief.

To loosen a cough and prevent it worrying a child there is nothing like a warm fruit drink. It can be home-made lemonade or orangeade, made with honey; or blackcurrant jam or syrup with added hot water, and if wished a little glycerine or olive oil. A spoonful of honey slowly sucked is also soothing to an irritated throat.

Sleeping on the side and with an extra pillow may prevent phlegm getting down the back of the throat and being swallowed. Warm feet are very important.

Help the children to spit up phlegm and not passively to swallow it and show them how to dispose of it. But do not take too much notice of a cough, for children so love limelight that they may develop a 'habit cough' just to win attention!

Poliomyelitis

Infantile Paralysis is by no means always easy to diagnose as its initial symptoms may be similar to other febrile attacks, though in some cases paralysis appears suddenly without previous warning. It is most prevalent in the late summer, when any child with headache, drowsiness, marked irritability, and especially pain or stiffness of neck of spine should at once be put to bed and kept quiet, isolated, and seen by a doctor. As a patient may be infectious several days before any signs or symptoms show themselves, anyone who had been in contact up to four days before the onset of the illness, should be in quarantine for three weeks. The incubation period lies as a rule between 7 and 14 days. Infection is passed on through personal contact, and the virus is found in nose, throat and bowels.

Whooping Cough

Difficult to diagnose at first, which is unfortunate as it is most infectious in the early stages. If there is an epidemic in the neighbourhood any contacts should be isolated for 3 weeks, though the incubation period may be considerably shorter than this. The cough gradually gets harder and noisier and becomes paroxysmal, the child getting red in the face with his exertion. Bouts may occur very frequently and, after about a fortnight, often end in the characteristic whoop, associated with a long indrawn breath. Though coughing may persist for 8 weeks or more, the infectious period is believed to be over after a month.

If vomiting occurs the child should be given a light meal to replace the loss, and soothing drinks should be at hand, such as blackcurrant syrup. Great care must be taken to avoid chilling, but in suitable weather the child can spend a large part of his time out-of-doors with advantage. The doctor will advise re vaccines, and the Homoeopathic practitioners have their special remedies both for prevention and cure.

Vaccination

Your doctor will advise about this. If it is done, the best time is about the end of the second month. A good site is on the chest, about 1 in. below the right nipple. This is easy to protect from accidental injury, and will not show in later life.

FOR FURTHER READING

First Aid in the Home. E. and S. Livingstone, 1s. 6d.

ABC of Nursing in the Home, by E. M. Gravelius. The British Red Cross Society, 2s. 6d.

Cure of Threadworms, from 'Mother and Home', 32, Southampton Street, London, W.C.2, 2½d. by post.

Infectious Diseases, from 'The Family Doctor', British Medical Association, Tavistock House, London, W.C.1, 4½d. by post.

Cassel's Family Doctor, 20s.

INFECTIOUS ILLNESSES

Infection	Incubation Period	Duration of Infection	Average Isolation Period	Description
Chicken Pox	14–21 days.	Until every scab off.	14 days.	Usually mild. Small reddish pimples, which fill with clear fluid, appear in successive crops and are intensely irritating. A soothing lotion and wearing of cotton gloves at night important.
Diphtheria	2–6 days.	2–4 weeks or until bacteriological examination of throat and throat negative.	According to doctor's advice.	Starts with headache, pallor, lassitude; sometimes difficulty in swallowing, and sore throat. Greyish spot or patches seen at back of the throat. No rash.
German Measles	17–18 days.	A week after onset of catarrh.	7 days.	Usually mild. Sudden onset. Rash appears as small pink spots on face and behind ears, spreading all over body. Fades within 48 hours as a rule. Eyes may be inflamed.
Measles	10–14 days.	During actual symptoms and for 5 days after appearance of rash.	14 days.	Starts with running eyes and nose and sneezing. Tiny whitish spots surrounded by red can be seen inside the mouth. Child out of sorts and irritable. Temperature raised. Rash appears on 3rd or 4th day, first on brow, later over body and limbs in red, roundish spots.
Mumps	12–26 days (usually 17–18 days).	Immediately prior to and during swelling of glands.	14 days.	The child is generally upset for a day or two before pain is felt about the angle of the jaw. The glands become swollen and tender; the jaws stiff and the saliva thick.
Scarlet Fever	3–5 days.	About 3 weeks or until any nose or ear discharge is cleared.	7 days after discharge from hospital.	Onset sudden with fever, sore throat, vomiting. Rash, finely spotted, evenly diffused and bright red, appears within 24 hours, first on neck and then spreading over trunk. Tongue becomes whitish with bright red spots. Rash lasts 3–10 days and then peels.
Whooping Cough	7–14 days.	4 weeks after start of whoop.	28 days from onset of whoop.	First symptoms that of head cold, with coughing worse at night. Characteristic whoop develops in about a fortnight.

Incubation Period is the interval between the infection beginning and signs appearing. *Isolation Period*, except where otherwise stated, is the duration of infection plus a few days safety margin.
Your doctor's advice should be followed in all cases.

XLV

FIRST AID

Bandaging

WHERE THERE HAS been any cut or bruise, a bandage will be necessary to hold a dressing in place, and to facilitate healing without infection. If a gauze roll is used, it is a good plan to fasten with a few strips of narrow adhesive to hold the bandage in place, especially with an active child. If adhesive plaster is used, do not overlap so that air can reach the area. Apply all bandages snugly but without risk of cutting off the circulation. If the wound throbs after the first 24 hours it is well to have a look at it and to show it to a doctor if necessary; but otherwise it is often best not to disturb the dressing until healing has taken place, applying a fresh outer covering when necessary. In removing the dressing, be careful not to pull the edges of the cut apart.

Bites and Stings

For midge bites, gently apply a little damp soap immediately, followed by dabbing with a cool lotion such as witch-hazel or calamine. The bee leaves its sting sticking to the skin and this must be removed. The best way is to pass a needle through a flame to sterilize and then gently extract. Afterwards dab the area with dilute ammonia, a moist blue bag, or baking soda (1 teaspoon to ½ pint), or smear lightly with honey. Do not rub for this would spread poison. For wasp stings, dab with dilute vinegar or lemon juice. A sting on the tongue necessitates hospital treatment. The tongue should, meanwhile, be kept forward.

Burns and Scalds

Slight burns with unbroken skin—relieve the local heat and disinfect by pouring Milton freely over the part. If this is not available, plunge affected part in cold water, or apply a cold wet cloth, renewing frequently.

Severe burns.—Summon the doctor. Treat for shock, not letting the child get hot which would increase discomfort. Luke-warm drinks, containing a little salt may be soothing. Avoid contamination by lightly covering the area with thoroughly clean material, such as the inside of freshly laundered linen. Do not apply oils or jellies, nor seek to cut away the clothing.

Bruises

A cold application, applied immediately, will ease pain; then apply firmly a bandage which has been wrung out of cold water; or squeeze a pad of cotton-wool in a tumbler of water to which one tablespoonful of methylated spirit has been added, apply and bandage.

Cuts

Cuts can be of differing degrees of severity. The mother should try to take time to wash her own hands before attending to them. The area must be well cleansed, using soap and running water. If a disinfectant is used, it should be a very mild one. Cold water tends to check bleeding; hot is more cleansing. Bleeding should not be stopped too soon as it helps to cleanse the wound. To control, raise the part affected, and press together the edges of the cut with dry cotton-wool. Afterwards these can be held together by the use of firm adhesive plaster cut into the shape of capital I's, with long top and bottom strips. To help the blood to clot, make a pad of folded linen or cotton-wool and apply pressure over this with the palm of the hand for 3 minutes and then release very gently.

In covering cuts, we must remember to allow for the normal evaporation of moisture from the skin. Grazes are best left exposed to the air.

Falls

As young children do not tense themselves when they fall, quite often they come to no harm. Providing there is no loss of consciousness after a fall on the head, and the child is soon comforted, there is, as a rule, nothing to worry about. Should there be loss of consciousness, vomiting, or signs of distress, a doctor should be called, and the child meanwhile kept flat in a darkened room, warmly covered, the head being kept to one side, in case of nausea. Nothing should be given by mouth.

Nose Bleeding

Though the amount lost is usually small it is often alarming to a child, so quiet reassurance is important. Lying down helps, as the action of the heart is then less forceful. Cold tends to constrict blood-vessels, and can be applied over the bridge of the nose, or at the nape of the neck, or ice be given to suck. If the bleeding point is low, to close the nostrils firmly with finger and thumb, holding until the blood has had time to clot, is the best plan.

Poisons

If your child has swallowed a poison, telephone the doctor and seek to make the child vomit, by slipping a finger down his throat, running it along the roof of the mouth, and down to the back of the throat, firmly but gently. Keep it there a few seconds, moving it to make him retch very thoroughly. To give a glass of milk, or water, first may be helpful, and will help to dilute the poison. After he has vomited, give him another drink and make him vomit again. Keep the child warm with hot-water bottles until the doctor comes.

Swallowed Objects

If these are smooth and rounded little harm will be done. Just watch the motions for a few days for the object to appear. In some cases it helps to give something stodgy and soft like porridge, bread, or a bun. Do not give a laxative, as in hurrying matters on it might cause the foreign body to graze the intestines. If the object is a sharp or dangerous one, such as an open safety-pin, consult your doctor at once.

FOR FURTHER READING

Emergency First Aid Chart, obtainable from 'Mother and Home', 32, Southampton Street, London, W.C.2, 2½d. by post.

XLVI

MATERNITY SERVICES AND BENEFITS

THE NATIONAL HEALTH SERVICE is a real boon to parents, for by its provisions the expectant mother gets her ante-natal care quite free, and, at the birth, has the services of doctor or midwife, or both where necessary. If the mother's usual doctor does not do maternity work he will pass her on to someone who undertakes this. If a hospital delivery is advised, this can be quite free, or the mother can make use of an amenity bed—if one is available and if she wishes the extra privacy—for a small charge.

The local Welfare Centre will advise on these and other matters as well as providing ante-natal care. In some Boroughs a maternity pack is provided free of charge. The services of a Home Help for a few weeks can also often be arranged for a small payment (or none if income is low).

Cash Grants

In leaflet No. 17, obtainable from local Pensions and National Insurance Offices, maternity cash benefits are set out clearly.

The main one is a £9 grant paid on the husband's, or the wife's, insurance (but not on both). Double for twins. Treble for triplets!

If the mother has been working, and is fully insured, with her card up to date for the year ending three months before the date of the expected confinement, she gets a maternity allowance of 32s. 6d. a week for 18 weeks, starting 11 weeks before the expected date. (No such allowance is paid if the wife is not insured, or only pays 3d. a week.)

If the confinement takes place at home, a special Confinement Grant of £3 is paid to cover various incidentals which would be provided in a hospital. This is payable on the wife's or the husband's insurance, not on both.

Make a point of sending in the claim forms in good time. This can be as early as 11 weeks before the expected confinement, or up to three months after it. Your doctor's or midwife's endorsement will, of course, be necessary.

Extra Milk and Vitamins

For the pregnant and nursing mother, and the young child, the special supplements originally offered as a war-time measure are still continued. The expectant mother should take the Certificate of Pregnancy, given to her by her doctor or midwife, to the local offices of the National Health Insurance, where she will be given a book of 26 tokens, and also the address where Welfare foods are available locally—usually the local Clinic.

Each token enables the mother to get 7 pints of milk, from her usual dairy, or one tin of National Dried milk, which, when reconstituted, makes up to the same amount, at special welfare prices.

Vitamins A and D tablets are available free to expectant mothers, and up to 30 weeks after the confinement, as an alternative to fresh cod-liver oil. The oil is also free for all children under school age; and concentrated orange juice is on sale for as little as 5*d.* a bottle.

APPENDIX

Apple Milk Shake

Take 2 tablespoons sweetened apple puree, whisk well in ½ pint fresh milk. Serve cold with a pinch of cinnamon or powdered cloves.

Apple Water Drink

Wash and dry apple, remove core. Grate apple, put into a jug, add a teaspoon of honey, a little lemon flavouring and a pint of boiling water. Cover jug. Strain when cool.

Note:—Apple-core, peel and pips, etc., covered with water, brought to boil, simmered 5 minutes, flavoured, makes a useful drink.

Barley or Oat Jelly

Mix 1 level tablespoon of Robinson's Patent Barley into a smooth paste with 2 oz. cold milk, add a pinch of salt and make up to 4 oz. by stirring in boiling water. Boil gently for 1–3 minutes. Serve warm, without sugar. Pour a little of the baby's milk mixture over the jelly.

Blackcurrant Drink

Puree, syrup, or jam may be used. Put one dessertspoon in a jug. Add 1 tablespoon lemon juice, and a small teaspoon honey. Pour over ½ pint boiling water and stir well. Cover, and leave near heat for 15–20 minutes. Strain.

Cottage Cheese

Place skimmed milk in a bowl; leave in a warm place till it thickens. Place a piece of cheese cloth or butter muslin over a cullender and stand the latter in a basin. Turn the thickened milk into this, tie up in the cloth and leave hanging over a basin until whey has drained off.

Custard (Baked)

Beat a fresh egg lightly and add to 6 oz. of milk and a teaspoon of sugar. Pour mixture into a small pie-dish. Stand this in a tin of cold water and set in a slow oven.

Appendix

Egg (*Coddled*)

Bring water to the boil. Slip in a fresh egg, cover, and stand saucepan to one side for about 5 minutes. The yolk will be nicely cooked and the white creamy and digestible.

Herring roes (*Creamed*)

2 herring roes, ¼ pint milk and water, ½ oz. flour, knob of margarine, or butter. Put roes in small saucepan with marg. and 2 ozs. of the milk and water. Stew very gently 10–15 minutes. Lift out roes and blend flour with remainder of milk, pour into saucepan, stirring until boiling. Cook 1–2 minutes. Add a little salt. Return roes to saucepan and bring again to boil.

Milk Jelly

Dissolve 1 oz. gelatine, or agar-agar, in hot water. Warm ¾ pint milk and add 1 tablespoon sugar. Add colouring and flavouring such as lemon or orange rind if wished. Add dissolved gelatine and stir in well. Pour into wetted mould and leave to set.

Muesli (*Health porridge*)

Soak 1 tablespoon oatmeal in 2 tablespoons of water or fruit juice until grain has swollen. Grate into this an unpeeled apple, including core. Add any other fruit, or fruit juice available, a dash of lemon juice, a teaspoon of honey, and one of nut cream or chopped nuts. Serve with a little top milk.

Rusks.

Cut stalish bread into slices ¾-in. thick and bake in a slow oven, with door ajar, until a deep cream colour.

Or, dip bread in milk, or Marmite and water (½ teaspoon to 1 tablespoon) before baking.

Or pull bread into uneven pieces and bake.

Note: To encourage baby to exercise his gums thoroughly and evenly different shaped rusks are valuable.

Vegetable Soup

Cut any vegetables available into small pieces after thorough cleansing. Cook in just sufficient boiling water to cover, simmering for about 20 minutes. Put through a sieve. Return to saucepan. Add a little milk and a knob of butter (vegetable extract if liked) and reheat.

VITAMIN TABLE

Name	Chief Functions	Chief Natural Sources
A	Anti-infective. Necessary for growth and development of teeth. Promotes health of mucous linings of respiratory tract. Increases night vision. Very important in childhood and pregnancy.	Fish liver oils, milk, butter, egg yolk, liver, carrots, spinach, fresh green vegetables, Bemax.
B (Complex)	This group of vitamins is not stored in the body, so daily intake needed. Promotes good nerves, appetite and digestion, also healthy skin. Deficiency leads to fatigue and irritability.	Yeast, whole cereals, the whole meal loaf, germ of wheat, peanuts, pulses, liver.
C	Necessary for healthy blood-vessels and blood-forming tissues, teeth, gums and bones. Increase important during infections. Living element easily lost and destroyed through cooking, storage, soaking, etc.	Found in most fresh fruits and vegetables, especially in blackcurrants, rose hips; oranges and lemons; in brussels sprouts, cauliflower, cabbage, watercress, etc.
$D_{1, 2}$	Promotes growth and formation of bones. Prevents rickets. Regulates calcium absorption. Especially necessary for mothers and growing children.	Fish liver oils, egg yolk. Produced by action of sunlight and ultra-violet rays on skin.
E	Promotes fertility. Prevents miscarriage.	Wheat germ oil, lettuce, liver, eggs.
K	Helps in the normal clotting of blood. Deficiency may cause haemorrhage.	Alfalfa and other green leaves, liver, fish, strawberries, rose hips.

HEIGHT AND WEIGHT TABLE

	Age						
	Birth	6 Mths.	1 Year	2 Yrs.	3 Yrs.	4 Yrs.	5 Yrs.
Height (ins.)	20–20½	26–26½	29	33–34	37–39	38–41	39–44
Weight (lbs.)	7–7½	15–16	20–21	26–27	31–32	35–37	37–45
Chest (ins.)	13–13½	16–16½	17½–18	18½–19½	19½–20	20–20½	20–21
Head (ins.)	13½–14	16½–17	17½–18	18½–19	19½	19½–20	20–21

SOCIETIES AND AGENCIES

HERE ARE SOME addresses of Societies interested in the care and well-being of parents and children. Special information and literature can be obtained from any of these:

National Association for Maternity and Child Welfare Centres, 5, Tavistock Place, London, W.C.1.

National Association for Mental Health, 39, Queen Anne Street, London, W.1.

National Baby Welfare Council, 31, Gloucester Place, London, W.1.

National Council for the Unmarried Mother and Her Child, 21, Coram Street, London, W.C.1.

National Marriage Guidance Council, 78, Duke Street, London, W.1.

National Society Prevention of Cruelty to Children, Victory House, Leicester Square, London, W.1.

National Society Children's Nurseries, 45, Russell Square, London, W.C.1.

The Nursery School Association of Gt. Britain, 1, Park Crescent, Portland Place, London, W.1.

British Homeopathic Association, 43, Russell Square, London, W.C.1.

Parents' National Educational Union, 171, Victoria Street, London, S.W.1.

Invalid Children's Aid Association, 4, Palace Gate, London, W.8.

Royal Society Prevention of Accidents, 52, Grosvenor Gardens, London, S.W.1.

Church of England Children's Society, Old Town Hall, Kennington, London, S.E.2.

The Nutrition Information Centre, Vitamins Limited, Upper Mall, London, W.6.

Oral Hygiene Service, Hesketh House, Portman Square, London, W.1.

Central Council for Health Education, Tavistock House, W.C.1.

Church of England Adoption Society, 4a, Bloomsbury Square, London, W.C.1.

National Children's Adoption Society, 71, Knightsbridge, London, S.W.1.

Family Welfare Association, 296, Vauxhall Bridge Road, London, S.W.1.

INDEX

Index

Hair, care of, 207; shampoo, 64, 207
Handicapped children, 198–200
Handkerchiefs, 214
Handling of young baby, 59
Head, shape of, 57, 58, 65; banging, 202
Heart burn, 38
Heat rash, 205; stroke, 105
Height, table of, 228
Hernia, 210
Hiccups, 210
Home Help Services, 44, 224

Imagination, 132, 146, 177, 189
Independence, 120, 161
Indigestion, 108
Infectious diseases, table of, 220
Inhaling, 212
Instincts, babies', 58
Invisible friend, 189–90
Iron, 9, 40; for premature, 150

Jaw exercise, 80, 86, 87, 137, 138
Jealousy, 161, 185–6, 201
Juices, 75–6, 84

Kariol, 82
Knock knee, 128, 210

Language development, 131–3
Laundry for baby, 155–7
Layettes, 26–30
Legs, swollen in pregnancy, 39; bowing of in child, 128
Length at birth, 2
Lice, 208
Loneliness, 108
Lying-in, 50–3

Manners, 192–3
Massage for prematures, 150, 151
Mastication, 86, 138, 139
Masturbation, 180, 202
Maternity Services and Benefits, 224–5
Maternity wear, 22–5
Mattress, for cot, 32, 33; for mother's bed 42
Measles, 220
Meat, 96
Meconium, 56
Mentally handicapped, 198–9
Milk, types of, 79; expressing, 20, 74; extra for mother, 225
Mineral salts, 9
Miscarriage, 41
Morning sickness, 38
Mothering, 58–60, 102, 109, 138, 146, 159
Mumps, 220
Muscle development, 116–17, 202

Nails, development before birth, 2; biting, 201
Names, choice of, 60–1
Napkin rash, 205
Napkins, method of applying, 66; giving up, 122; washing, 156
Natural childbirth, 13
Negativism, 146–7
Nervous system, babies, 59; habits, 201–3
New born baby, 55–60
Night feed, 102, 103

Nipples, preparation of, 19–20; cracked or sore, 70
Nits, 208
Nose, breathing, 64, 109; bleeding, 223; cleaning, 64
Nursery furnishing, 31–7
Nuts, 96, 97

Obedience, 145–6
Odd man out, 191
Only child, 192
Orange juice, 76, 79, 225
Over-feeding, 71, 107, 108
Ovum, 1

Pain, relief of, 46
Parent-child relationship, 158–62, 197
Pelvis, 15, 16, 46, 51
Perambulator, choice and care of, 36, 37
Pets, 173, 176, 184
Phantasies, invisible friend, 189
Physical skills, 118–19, 173
Picnics, 119
Pigmentation, 4
Pilches, 28
Play, in infancy, 169; parallel, 188; educative, 171; active, 173
Playmates, 188–9
Play-pen, 102
Pocket-money, 174–5
Poisons, 223
Poliomyelitis, 218
Possessiveness, 161
Pregnancy, signs of, 3 ;duration of, 5; tests for, 5; rules of health for, 7–18
Premature babies, 149–51
Proteins, 8, 95, 96, 97, 98
Punishment, 164–7
Purees, 84, 85

Quarantine, 220
Quarrels, 184, 192
Questions, 132, 176, 177, 178, 196
Quickening, 5

Rashes, 205
Raspberry leaf tea, 10
Raw foods, 8
Recipes, 82, 226–7
Relaxation, 11, 13, 46, 47; in children, 114
Religious training, 113, 194–6
Rest, for mother, 73, 100; for child, 111, 114
Rh factor, 6
Routine, for baby, 100–3; for toddler, 103
Rupture, 210
Rusks, 86, 227

Safe period, 54
Safety gate, 118; strap, 36
Scalds, 221
Scales, 36, 74
Scalp, care of, 206–7
Scarlet Fever, 220
Screen, 35
Scurf, 57, 207
Security, 58, 59, 109, 121, 186, 188
Self-consciousness, 109, 112, 158, 188
Self-control, 121, 148
Senses, development of, 170, 180
Sex determination, 6; differences, 160–1; education, 177–80; play, 180

231

Index